CAMBRIDGE LIBRARY COLLECTION

Books of enduring scholarly value

Spiritualism and Esoteric Knowledge

Magic, superstition, the occult sciences and esoteric knowledge appear regularly in the history of ideas alongside more established academic disciplines such as philosophy, natural history and theology. Particularly fascinating are periods of rapid scientific advances such as the Renaissance or the nineteenth century which also see a burgeoning of interest in the paranormal among the educated elite. This series provides primary texts and secondary sources for social historians and cultural anthropologists working in these areas, and all who wish for a wider understanding of the diverse intellectual and spiritual movements that formed a backdrop to the academic and political achievements of their day. It ranges from works on Babylonian and Jewish magic in the ancient world, through studies of sixteenth-century topics such as Cornelius Agrippa and the rapid spread of Rosicrucianism, to nineteenth-century publications by Sir Walter Scott and Sir Arthur Conan Doyle. Subjects include astrology, mesmerism, spiritualism, theosophy, clairvoyance, and ghost-seeing, as described both by their adherents and by sceptics.

The Book of Protection

Sir Hermann Gollancz (1852–1930) was an English rabbi, scholar and public figure whose distinguished career led to his becoming the first rabbi to receive a knighthood. Gollancz was Professor of Hebrew at University College London from 1902 to 1924 and published extensively on Jewish history as well as translating many Hebrew and Aramaic texts. This 1912 volume contains editions, with translations and notes, of three Syriac manuscripts (two from Gollancz' personal library and a third from Cambridge University Library) containing a collection of Eastern Christian charms and incantations. They range from antidotes to headaches, colic and 'teeth chattering' to prayers for controlling mad dogs, unruly cows and 'the gun of warriors', as well as for warding off the evil eye. They begin with the Trinitarian formula and often invoke specific biblical stories to add force. Illustrations from Codex A (dated to 1802 and from Turkish Kurdistan) are also included.

T0370568

Cambridge University Press has long been a pioneer in the reissuing of out-of-print titles from its own backlist, producing digital reprints of books that are still sought after by scholars and students but could not be reprinted economically using traditional technology. The Cambridge Library Collection extends this activity to a wider range of books which are still of importance to researchers and professionals, either for the source material they contain, or as landmarks in the history of their academic discipline.

Drawing from the world-renowned collections in the Cambridge University Library, and guided by the advice of experts in each subject area, Cambridge University Press is using state-of-the-art scanning machines in its own Printing House to capture the content of each book selected for inclusion. The files are processed to give a consistently clear, crisp image, and the books finished to the high quality standard for which the Press is recognised around the world. The latest print-on-demand technology ensures that the books will remain available indefinitely, and that orders for single or multiple copies can quickly be supplied.

The Cambridge Library Collection will bring back to life books of enduring scholarly value (including out-of-copyright works originally issued by other publishers) across a wide range of disciplines in the humanities and social sciences and in science and technology.

The Book of Protection

Being a Collection of Charms

EDITED BY HERMANN GOLLANCZ

CAMBRIDGE
UNIVERSITY PRESS

CAMBRIDGE UNIVERSITY PRESS

Cambridge, New York, Melbourne, Madrid, Cape Town, Singapore,
São Paolo, Delhi, Dubai, Tokyo, Mexico City

Published in the United States of America by Cambridge University Press, New York

www.cambridge.org
Information on this title: www.cambridge.org/9781108027748

© in this compilation Cambridge University Press 2010

This edition first published 1912
This digitally printed version 2010

ISBN 978-1-108-02774-8 Paperback

THE BOOK OF PROTECTION

THE
BOOK OF PROTECTION

BEING A COLLECTION OF CHARMS

NOW EDITED FOR THE FIRST TIME
FROM SYRIAC MSS.

WITH TRANSLATION, INTRODUCTION, AND NOTES

BY

HERMANN GOLLANCZ, M.A., D.Lit.

GOLDSMID PROFESSOR OF HEBREW
UNIVERSITY COLLEGE, LONDON

WITH 27 ILLUSTRATIONS

LONDON
HENRY FROWDE
OXFORD UNIVERSITY PRESS, AMEN CORNER, E.C.
1912

OXFORD: HORACE HART
PRINTER TO THE UNIVERSITY

CONTENTS

INTRODUCTION

In these introductory remarks I propose to limit myself to a description, with a few explanatory notes and details, of the two Syriac MSS. in my possession, published for the first time in this form. They were first brought to public notice at the International Congress of Orientalists held at Paris in 1897, on which occasion I read a paper entitled, 'A Selection of Charms from Syriac Manuscripts,' which was later on included in the *Actes du onzième Congrès International des Orientalistes*. The interest which this paper evoked at the time, and the repeated requests made to me since, have encouraged me to carry out at last both my own wish and the wish of others, that I should publish the text and translation of these MSS. in their entirety. I might add that as far as concerns the libraries I have been able to consult, these MSS. are extremely rare. The British Museum came into possession of one almost identical with the larger of the two but a few years ago, and the Cambridge University Library has one MS. similar to the smaller one, but smaller still, the writing being nothing near so clear and careful, nor the illustrations so good. It is described at fair length in William Wright's *Catalogue of the Syriac Manuscripts preserved in the Library of the University of Cambridge*, 1901.

It was my intention at first simply to make this reference to Wright's *Catalogue*, and leave the reader to consult and compare the Cambridge MS. But upon consideration, observing the important discrepancies between this MS. and my smaller one, I have determined to include in this volume the full text of the Cambridge MS., together with a translation.

b

As regards my own two MSS., the one which I now call Codex A is larger in size and contains a much larger number of incantations, &c., whilst the smaller, which I call Codex B, is older, and what is most valuable, it has the vowel signs throughout; thus leaving little doubt as to the pronunciation especially of the proper names cited therein. Both contain illustrations more or less crude, but yet of undoubted interest; the headings in both are in red, the main portion in black: and they are written on paper.

The Cambridge MS. I call Codex C, and in the Appendix I have added some interesting details with reference to the collation of the British Museum MS., which I cite as B.M.

Codex A is dated '2114 of the blessed Greeks', which corresponds to the year 1802–3. It consists of seventy-two pages of text and two additional pages with illustrations at end, which I have divided into fifty-four sections (§), following more or less indications in the text. The writing approximates to Estrangelo; the place in which it was written is Shibani, among the mountains of Turkish Kurdistan, two days' ride from Urmiah.

On the two blank pages in front of the MS. there occur the following inscriptions in pencil with the name of the owner, ܓܝܘܪܓܝܣ ܒܪ ܠܥܙܪ Georgis bar Lazar, while the name (spelt thus) ܓܝܘܪܓܝܣ ܒܪ ܠܵܥܵܙܵܪ is also once in ink:—

(a) ܗܢܐ ܟܬܒܐ ܕܝܘܣܦ ܩܪܝܬܐ ܕܚܡܩܝ ܐܬܝܗܒ
ܡܢ ܝܘܣܦ ܒܪ ܡܪܓܘܠ ܩܪܝܬܐ ܕܐܒܓܠܘ 1889

'This book belongs to Joseph of the village of Chamaki; it was given by Joseph son of Margul, of the village of Abajalu, 1889.'

(b) ܐܢܐ ܐܘܓܠܝܛܐ:
ܦܫܘܛ ܡܪܝ ܘܐܠܗܝ ܡܫܝܚܐ ܕܪܚܡܢܘܬܟ ܡܢ
ܪܘܡܐ ܕܩܘܕܫܐ ܗܘ ܒܐܘܠܨܢܐ ܕܫܘܠܛܢܟ ܥܘܕܪܢܗ
ܠܐܡܬܐ ܡܣܟܢܬܐ ܕܡܪܘܬܟ

Lo the Evangelist!

'Stretch forth, O my Lord and God, the right hand of Thy compassion from the High Sanctuary. Grant the food of those who worship Thee—an abundance of the heavenly grace of Thy sovereignty.'

This is the ordinary Chaldaic prayer before meals.

On the last page the following occurs (in ink) in a third hand:—

(c) ܗܕܐ ܟܬܒܬܐ ܕܡܝܪܙܐ ܒܪ ܣܗܕܐ ܡܢܝܚܐ
ܠܓܝܘܪܓܝܣ ܐܝܬ (modern for ܡܢ) ܡܒܓܠܘܐ ܓܒܪܐ ܕܒܐܝܕܗ
ܒܐܕܗ (sic) ܠܐ ܡܕܪܐ ܠܡܪܘܗ (sic) ܗܘܐ ܬܚܝܬ
ܚܪܡܐ ܕܡܪܝ ܫܡܥ[ܘܢ].

'This MS. (is the property) of Mirza son of the deceased martyr George from Abajalu [two hours' walk from Urmiah]. The man in whose hand it will fall and he will not return it to its owner, may he be under the ban of Mar Simeon.'

Codex B is very small in size, consisting of 118 pages carefully written in Estrangelo proper, nine lines to a page; and, as I have remarked before, it has the vowel signs throughout. Particular attention should be called to the large number of Fathers and Saints occurring in § 5, some perhaps hitherto scarcely or not at all known, many more than the number mentioned in the corresponding incantation in Codex A, § 52.

Codex C (in the words of Wright) is written in an inelegant Nestorian, probably of the eighteenth century, and I might add that, in proportion to its size, it contains a large number of scribe's errors. A striking instance is to be found in § 11, more especially when compared with B.M. § 55.

As regards the texts of A and B, the MSS. are in the main correctly written: scribes' errors are pointed out in footnotes to the passages as they occur. Headings and other expressions

in red in the originals are represented by the bold type in
the Syriac portion of this volume. Codex B is printed line
for line according to the original, and the number of pages
(118) is also indicated.

As far as the meaning of some few passages is concerned,
they practically baffle all satisfactory interpretation; perhaps
this was the intention of the author of the charm. Yet, in
one or two instances, instead of leaving them untranslated,
as was my original intention, a tentative translation is offered
as the basis of a more complete rendering.

The first instance is Cod. A, § 19. We have there, in the
latter half especially, an admixture of Syriac, Arabic, and
other expressions, which admits of no easy explanation.

Similarly in the case of § 41, referring to the Ring of
King Solomon, the names therein contained must I fear
remain inexplicable, for they are evidently mystical names.
But it may be of interest to note the recurrence of the
syllable מִץ and פִּץ in combination and permutation. And
here we have some light thrown upon the subject from the
fact that מצפ״ץ occurs in other works of a similar nature as
a transposition of letters for the Tetragrammaton (JHVH)
יהוה according to the principle א״ת ב״שׁ, i. e. the interchange
of the first and last letter, the second and last but one letter,
and so on of the Hebrew alphabet. Thus: מ would stand
for J, צ for H, פ for V and ץ for H—hence יהוה (JHVH).

It is further interesting to find the term פצפ״ציה applied
to the 'great Angel' appointed as the champion of Israel on
the day on which the 'Cornet' is blown. Here we have פץ
reduplicated, added to the terminal יה (Jah), which is the
shorter name for the 'Eternal'.

So far for the *names* on the RING OR SEAL OF SOLOMON.
But as regards the story itself and the power of Solomon
over the spirits and the animal kingdom, we have ample
references in Semitic literature. We read it e. g. in the
Talmud, Treatise *Gittin*, 68 a–b; it occurs in somewhat

different form in the *Midrash Tehillim* on Psalm lxxviii. 45, again in the *Yalkut Shimoni*, 1 Kings vi.

In the Koran (ch. xxxviii) we have a brief reference to it (*see* Note to Sale's edition).

The part which King Solomon plays in the history of Magic generally may further be gleaned from the description which I published of the Hebrew MS. in my possession, dated 1700 (according to the title-page, which may be later than the copy itself) called מפתח שלמה 'Clavicula Salomonis' (1903). The special reference to Ashmodai will be found on pp. 33, 34.

Coming to more modern works, I would further refer the reader to the valuable articles in Hamburger's *Real-Encyclopädie für Bibel und Talmud*, vol. II, on 'Geister', 'Ashmedai', &c.; to the chapter on 'Solomon and the Queen of Saba' in Weil's *The Bible, the Koran, and the Talmud : Biblical Legends*, &c. (1846); to M. A. Levy's scholarly 'Epigraphische Beiträge' in the *Jahrbuch für die Geschichte der Juden* (1861), pp. 267–271 and 294–295; to the full articles in the *Jewish Encyclopedia* on 'Solomon' and the 'Seal of Solomon'. See also M. Grünbaum's *Neue Beiträge zur Semitischen Sagenkunde* (1893), pp. 201, 211 sqq.; Eliphas Lévi's *Transcendental Magic* (ed. Waite, 1896).

But perhaps, after all, the crucial version of this much involved story may be found in the early statement of Josephus in his *Antiquities of the Jews*, Bk. VIII, ch. ii, § 5 ; and I will therefore reproduce it here, both on account of its antiquity and its terseness :—

'Now the sagacity and wisdom which God had bestowed on Solomon was so great, that he exceeded the ancients in so much that he was no way inferior to the Egyptians, who are said to have been beyond all men in understanding; nay, indeed, it is evident that their sagacity was very inferior to that of the king's. He also excelled and distinguished himself in wisdom above those who were most eminent among the Hebrews at that time for shrewdness : those I mean were Ethan, and Heman, and Chalcol, and Darda, the sons of

Mahol. He also composed books of odes and songs, a thousand
and five; of parables and similitudes, three thousand; for he
spake a parable on every sort of tree, from the hyssop to the
cedar; and in like manner also about beasts, about all sorts
of living creatures, whether upon the earth, or in the seas,
or in the air; for he was not unacquainted with any of their
natures, nor omitted enquiries about them, but described them
all like a philosopher, and demonstrated his exquisite knowledge of their several properties. God also enabled him to
learn that skill which expels demons, which is a science useful
and sanative to men. He composed such incantations also
by which distempers are alleviated. And he left behind him
the manner of using exorcisms, by which they drive away
demons so that they never return, and this method of cure
is of great force unto this day; for I have seen a certain
man of my own country whose name was Eleazar, releasing
people who were demoniacal in the presence of Vespasian
and his sons, and his captains, and a whole multitude of his
soldiers. The manner of the cure was this:—He put a ring
that had a root of one of those sorts mentioned by Solomon
to the nostrils of the demoniac, after which he drew out the
demon through his nostrils; and when the man fell down
immediately, he abjured him to return into him no more,
making still mention of Solomon, and reciting the incantations
which he composed. And when Eleazar would persuade and
demonstrate to the spectators that he had such a power, he
set a little way off a cup or basin full of water, and commanded the demon as he went out of the man to overturn it,
and thereby to let the spectators know that he had left the
man, and when this was done, the skill and wisdom of
Solomon was shewn very manifestly: for which reason it is,
that all men may know the vastness of Solomon's abilities,
and how he was beloved of God, and that the extraordinary
virtues of every kind with which this king was endowed may
not be unknown to any people under the sun; for this reason,
I say, it is that we have proceeded to speak so largely of
these matters.'

In connexion with this ancient version, the following
extracts from a remarkable anonymous pamphlet, entitled
The Talisman (printed by W. Whaley, 12 Holywell Street,
Strand, no date) may be read with interest:—

'Tyrant! (p. 9) I have tarried, I have wielded a power of the
thousand powers which may not resist the word of authority
spoken by him who has looked unmoved and unrebuked upon

the glories of the Shechinah, who has lifted the vail of the temple, penetrated into the Holy of Holies, and learned the words of power engravened upon *the signet of the master of all wisdom and of all demons*—good or evil—*the marvellous, the glorious Solomon.'*

'And yet (pp. 11, 12) it is perfectly true that it is the quality of this root, as is averred by sundry writers of our despised and persecuted race to cast out evil demons from people possessed—and though it is never known to more than one person of our race, a preparation of this root (Baara) aided by the words of might engraven upon *the signet of Solomon* is potent exceedingly in tasking the hidden powers and in discovering the most hidden things.' 'The all-but-omnipotent signet of Solomon was deposited by that greatest of earthly princes in the Temple of Jerusalem; and in the Holy of Holies, entered only by the great High-Priest, reposed that gem of price and power unspeakable.'

Nebuchadnezzar and Cyrus bore away the wealth of Jerusalem, but not this signet ring, 'which was from the beginning destined to work out the salvation of Judah, when her sins should be fully expiated and her people once more an acceptable people in the sight of the Lord.' It was successively preserved by each High Priest to the time of Titus: at the burning of the Temple the High Priest enjoins our magician with his dying breath to penetrate the Holy of Holies and snatch therefrom Solomon's signet ring, ' to snatch thence and from the very centre of the ark the Talisman of our people, even *the signet of the wise Solomon,* the Shem-ama-phorah (*sic* !) ' . . . . 'It (the ark, p. 16) was five spans long by three in height and breadth, and was strongly ornamented with plates of fine gold, and on the top were two cherubims of like precious metal. In that lay the palladium of our people—*the seal of Solomon;* and I, I! was to stretch forth my hand and seize it! The lid of the ark yielded to my mere touch and mine eyes fell upon the precious signet. It consisted of a single cincture of massive gold, set with a single gem : but such a gem ! In the centre of the gem was engraven the ineffable name of God, and around it in mingled

radiance of diamond, of sapphire, of ruby and emerald, the seeming of 10,000 eyes gleamed with divine ardour, to which the lurid lightnings of the stormiest heaven are but as a meteor that dances upon the morass.' He seizes the ring just as he hears Titus approaching, but feels himself grasped by a giant hand and loses consciousness. When he recovers he finds himself under a palm, by the side of a fountain seated amidst wonderful surroundings, and listening to heavenly music. But *Solomon's ring* has gone. He is in the greatest grief at the discovery; but a voice from above soothes him and assures him that the ring is destined to play a great rôle in the history of his persecuted race. 'Words of might were engraven upon my soul, even the words of *the signet of Solomon* which all genii must obey, and I was sent forth to live the bodily life and die the bodily death in divers places—but with ever one task, one trust,' &c.

Intimately bound up with the lore of the magician was the science of numbers.

Now as regards the inherent numerical value of the letters of the Hebrew alphabet, we would quote the following from 'The York Medal, or the supposed Jewish Medal found in York', deciphered by Dr. L. Loewe, and extracted from the *York Courant* (1843) :—

'Ibn Ezra in his work, *Sefer Hashem*, says with reference to the numerical importance of the letters *Alef*, *Hé*, *Wav*, and *Yod* (אהוי) which compose the great name, the Tetragrammaton and the *Éhé* (Exodus ch. iii, ver. 14), "These letters are peculiarly adapted for the purpose, as they surpass, in their capabilities, all the rest of the alphabet." . . . The numerical value of *Hé* and *Yod* is 15, which corresponds with the word composed of *Yod* and *Hé*, denoting God. The letter *Hé* alone, not followed by *Yod*, would, on having joined to it the four preceding numbers, produce the number 15, which is again the numerical value of the word composed of *Yod* and *Hé*, signifying God, thus $1+2+3+4+5=15$. . . . The four numbers, 1, 5, 6, 10 (אהוי) are denominated to distinguish them from the others, "round numbers" (*numeri rotundi*). This was done, probably, because they always re-appear in

their products, whether multiplied in the square or cube, having, figuratively, the properties of a circle, and the letters expressing the name of the Most Holy, being such as correspond, in their numerical value, to those now referred to, are used to represent, emblematically, His *perfection, immutability,* and *infinity.*

'The number 9 was said to be perfect in itself, because it involves the products of all the preceding numbers when multiplied. . . .

'The numbers 9 and 15 were adopted, therefore, to represent the attributes of the Deity; "for", said the teachers, "the number 9, multiplied in every way, is immutable, and always produces a number to (*sic!*) exact proportion to its simple value". . . . In Hebrew the word "truth" is thus emblematically conveyed, the simple numerical value of its characters being 9, intimating that *truth* never changes. The word is Emét (אמת), and is composed of the letters *Alef* (א) 1, *Mim* (מ) 40, *Tav* (ת) 400; and by taking the tens and hundred as units 1, 4, 4, we produce, by adding them together, 9. In Hebrew, the word signifying *man* is also composed of letters that represent numbers, which, if added together on the same plan, amount to the value of 9; for Adam (אדם), "man", is composed of *Alef* (א) 1, *Dalet* (ד) 4, and *Mim* (מ) 40; and by taking the figures, which stand for tens as units, 1 + 4 + 4, the product is 9 (vide Irira in his work *Sháar Hashámáyîm*).

'The number 15 has already been shown to correspond to the name of the Deity, composed of *Yod* and *Hé.* The tablet bearing an inscription of 9 and 15, a plan of which is here given, is considered the most ancient of its sort, and is therefore denominated, "*The seal of Solomon*".

ו	ז	ב		6	7	2
א	ה	ט		1	5	9
ח	ג	ד		8	3	4

'The number 9 is represented by the nine compartments; and the figures are so ranged in every line of the three compartments, whether horizontal, vertical, or diagonal, that the

number 15 is produced by adding together the numbers contained in the three compartments.

'So far, it must be seen, that such tablets were designated for no other purpose than to keep the minds of their possessors constantly dwelling on the words "God of Truth"; that whoever believed in the "God of Truth" might discard the fear of every other object known to them, the influence of charms and of stars and planets included. It was natural to suppose that the possessor of such a tablet would continually meditate on the attributes of the Omniscient, and bear in mind the universe was the work of His hands, and in every respect perfectly subordinate to Him; that His actions were all based in truth, and that whatever emanated from Him bore the stamp of truth and harmony.

'But whilst tablets and scrolls thus inscribed had a beneficial effect on those to whom their use was correctly explained, they produced mischief to those who could not interpret their meaning, and such, instead of contemplating, through them, the true nature of the Divinity, and estimating as they ought to have done all inferior objects, their ideas became distorted, and they looked upon the senseless pieces of metal or parchment containing mystical inscriptions as though they were charms in themselves, invested with power to counterbalance the influence of adverse planets or other charms, and this conception, aided by degrees by the practices of necromante impostors, unknown and mystical inscriptions were multiplied on various substances to an immense extent, and largely distributed to the inferior portions of society. Square tablets, or signets, were fabricated, with inscriptions having allusion to each of the planets; and in process of time similar articles were produced, to suit an infinite variety of purposes, all widely different from the sacred one for which such things were first invented.'

So far the value of numbers as represented by the letters of the Hebrew alphabet, and their relation to the Seal or Signet of Solomon.

Speaking of Solomon, we pass on to an expression which occurs in the present volume, and which may at first sight seem difficult of explanation; I refer to the appellation in § 35, SOLOMON BAR JAKI. What is the meaning of *bar Jaki*?

On reference to Proverbs, ch. xxxi. 1, we find these words: דברי אגור בן יקה 'The words of Agur the son of Jakeh.'

This clause has given rise to a deal of discussion, and it has been explained thus :—' Agur ' is another name for Solomon, אגור שאגר דברי תורה, who had ' collected ', ' stored up ' (rt. אגר) knowledge and experience, and afterwards had ' given them up ' (lit. ' spewed them out '; rt. קוא or קיא, cf. Lev. xviii. 25, 28, xx. 22 ; Jonah ii. 11 ; Job x. 15 ; Prov. xxiii. 18), for the benefit of mankind as maxims and rules of conduct to guide them in life; in another sense, Solomon had ' given them up ', i. e. ' had renounced them ' (יקה שהקיא דברי תורה) כספל הזה שהוא מתמלא בין שעתו ומתפנה בין שעתו Midrash *Koheleth* I, 1). Note also that the Vulgate renders the phrase : ' Verba Congregantis filii Vomentis.'

This latter explanation would be parallel to one of the interpretations given to the words in the next chapter of Proverbs, lxxxi. 1, דברי למואל מלך ' the words of Lemuel king '. Why is Solomon called Lemuel (למואל) ? Because there were occasions in life on which he threw off the yoke of Heaven and denied God, saying, למה לו אל ' Wherefore do I require God ? ' Of course others explain it again in the contrary sense, למו אל, Solomon was the one ' to whom God ' was all in all—in fact, a correlative of the name Jedidiah, ' beloved of the Lord ' (2 Sam. xii. 25).

This is not the place to enter deeply into questions of etymology, or to discuss the question in its entire bearing. It has, for example, been objected that not the past participle אגור, but the present participle אוגר (cf. Proverbs x. 5 אוגר בקיץ ' He who gathers in summer ', &c.) should have been used, if it was to have applied to Solomon. But we dare not forget that we have such forms in an active sense, as e. g. יקוש ' the fowler ' (Ps. xci. 3).

Then again it has been asked : Why call *David* Jakeh ? But the rejoinder is: Jakeh is applied not to David but to Solomon himself ; and the word בֵּן is not ' son of ', but it is used in the same sense as בן שנה ' one a year old ', בן שמן ' one oily ', i. e. ' fertile ' (Isaiah v. 1) ; thus the phrase

בן יקה would mean 'one who spewed out', 'gave out' or
'renounced'.

Suffice it to say, however, that the expression exists in
Scripture in the form 'Agur, the son of Jakeh', and this is
sufficient to account for its introduction into the wording of
our text.

There occurs in A, § 20, the expression ܙܘܥܐ ܕܠܒܐ,
which may be rendered either 'wind of the heart', i.e. cramp
or rheumatism, or more literally still, having in view the
purpose of this work, 'THE SPIRIT' or 'DEMON' of the heart.

This opens up a very wide subject of engrossing interest
to the student of Oriental literature. As far as concerns
Eastern popular custom, influenced by Chaldaic and Babylonian
currents, all ailments were looked upon as caused by specific
'demons' or 'evil spirits', and among the Jews of many
centuries these were called by such names as שׁדים, מזיקים,
רוחות, &c. It is therefore not surprising to find in the
Talmud, Treatise *Gittin*, 67 b, on the phrase מי שׁאחזו
קרדייקום, both the Talmud itself and the eminent com-
mentator Rashi explaining the word קרדייקום by שׁר or
שׁם שׁידה 'demon' or 'the name of a female demon', though
we recognize it as καρδιακός (=καρδιαλγής, καρδιαλγία)
'heart-ache' (also 'stomachic pains'). In the same manner
'leprosy' is identified with the demon 'Ḥamat' (*Sanhedrin*,
101 a), 'asthma' or 'melancholy' with the spirit 'Ben
Nephalim' (*Bechoroth*, 44 b), 'throat affections' among
children with 'Shibbeta' (*Taanith*, 20 b), &c.

Coming from 'DEMONS' to 'THE SERPENT' to which somewhat frequent reference is made in these texts, I will quote
the following from Grünbaum (p. 61): In the various
passages of the Koran in which mention is made of the
enticing of Adam and his wife (who, by the way, is not
mentioned by name, Sur. 2, 34; 7, 19 sq., 20, 118 sq.) the

serpent is not spoken of; Satan is the seducer. As, however, the question arose as to how the latter could have entered Paradise, once having been expelled thence by God (Sur. 2, 34; 7, 19; 38, 78), Zamahśarî notes on Sur. 2, 34 *that having concealed himself in the mouth of the Serpent*, he entered Paradise; whilst Baidâwî adduces further explanations.

The Koran accordingly follows in this matter not the Jewish but the Syro-Christian tradition.

Compare in this connexion Weil's *Biblical Legends*, ch. i, pp. 7–15. In the course of his remarks on the subject we read:—'How can I bring thee into Paradise unobserved?' inquired the serpent. 'I will contract myself into so small a bulk that I shall find room in the cavity of thy teeth.' ... The serpent then opened her mouth—Iblis ('the master of all evil spirits') flew into it, and seating himself in the hollow of her front teeth poisoned them to all eternity (p. 10).

I might here state that, as far as references in the Talmud to magic and its practice is concerned, the chief sources of information are to be found in the Treatises *Pesaḥim*, 110–112; *Sabbath*, 66–67; *Sanhedrin*, 65 a–67, 111; *Gittin*, 67 b, 70 a; and *Ḥulin*, 105 b, 109.

But the history of magic in general, its origin and development,—the consideration of charms, incantations, amulets and exorcisms,—this vast subject cannot be treated within the limits of a brief Introduction.

And as regards Syrian Magic, the specimens contained in the present volume may now be allowed to speak for themselves; and it must be left to the student to discover how far they are original in thought, or to what extent they have been affected by influences derived from adjacent peoples.

As to the illustrations in our MSS.:—In Codex A we have on p. 1 of the text a horse-shoe border or vignette; on p. 3, a square divided into thirty-six smaller spaces, containing

the words of St. John i ; on p. 4, representations of ' Matthew '
' Mark ', ' Luke ', and ' John '; on p. 6, a picture of ' Mar
Georgis' on horseback and 'the great dragon'; on p. 11,
figures with the description, 'This is the ruler executing
judgment', with his 'pipe', 'sword', 'purse', 'goose', and
' fire'; on p. 15 we have representations of various implements,
such as ' bow and arrows ', ' club ', ' hatchet ', ' gun ', ' sword ',
' daggers '; on p. 17, in the centre, a star or Catherine-wheel ;
p. 20, equestrian figure of ' Mar Thomas ' engaging with ' the
Spirit of Lunacy '; p. 24, pictures of various animals, ' ram '
or ' stag ', ' goat ', ' he-goat ', ' hare ', ' fox ', ' sparrow ', and
' fowl '; on p. 27, various kinds of ' guns '; on p. 34, ' the
Angel Gabriel ' on horseback in an encounter with the ' Evil
Eye '; p. 39, an equestrian figure of ' Rabban Hurmizd ' with
an animal to which is affixed the description, ' This is a lion
or a mad dog '; on p. 47, ' Daniel the prophet ' on horse with
' the cunning wolf lying in ambush for the sheep '; p. 49,
picture of ' two serpents ', and on p. 50 of ' two scorpions ';
p. 54 contains circle with inscription round the border in illustration of the ' Seal of Solomon ', and on p. 55 ' King Solomon '
himself seated on a horse in an encounter with ' Ashmedai ';
on p. 58 appears ' Mar Shalita ' riding against the ' Evil
Spirit '. The whole of p. 64 is taken up with two figures
seated on thrones, one ' Elias ', the other ' Enoch ', on either
side of a tree with fruit (evidently guarding Paradise) ; pp. 73
and 74 contain fanciful illustrations of a star and a cross;
pp. 17, 35, 36, 55, and 56, have at the foot of the page the
letters ܐ, ܒ, ܓ, ܕ, ܗ respectively.

Codex B has also on first page a vignette border ; on p. 23
a crude illustration of a hero on horse without description,
evidently fighting the Evil Spirit; on p. 57, woman on horse
described ' This is Mary, the mother of Christ ', with figure,
having the words, ' This is the wicked Satan '; on p. 71, ' Mar
'Abd-īshō' ' (equestrian) and ' the accursed Satan '; p. 86, 'This
is Mar Georgis ' (on horse), and on p. 95 an illustration of

'the Evil Eye'. The pp. 17, 18, 37, 38, 58, 77, 78, 97, and 98 have at foot the letters ܐ, ܒ, ܓ, ܕ, ܗ, ܗ, ܚ, ܚ, ܛ respectively.

Codex C has on p. 4 b illustration of the 'wicked demon'; on p. 8 a, a cross within a circle; p. 11 a, 'Mar Georgis and the dragon'; p. 13 b, a circle; p. 19 b, an 'Emir with pipe, sword, axe, &c.'; p. 23 b, 'Mar Milis and the ox'; p. 25 b, 'Mar Hananiah and tiger'; p. 26 a, 'circle'; p. 27 b, ornamentation; p. 31 a, star within circle; p. 33 b, 'Mar Moushé (on horse) and the devil'; p. 37 a, four doves' heads in a circle; p. 39 a, 'Mar Joseph and the wicked person'; p. 41 a, cross in circle; p. 43 a, 'This is an olive-tree'; p. 45 b, 'Mar Daniel, bear and dove'; p. 50 b, 'Mar Joseph and Lilith'; p. 52 b, a wheel; p. 58 a, 'Mar Gabriel and the Evil Eye'; p. 61 a, circle; p. 63 a, scorpions; p. 65 b, 'These are serpents'; p. 68 a, 'Lion, goat, fox and hare'; p. 70 a, 'Mar 'Abd-īshō' and the accursed devil'; p. 72 b, fanciful illustration; p. 76 a, 'Enoch and Elias' on each side of a tree; p. 80 b, 'Mar Sabarishō' and the Satan'; p. 83 a, 'guns and flints'; p. 84 a, illustration of 'Shield of David'.

It remains for me to thank several friends for their kind suggestions and ready assistance while this book was passing through the press, more especially the veteran Orientalist, Professor Th. Nöldeke of Strassburg, Professor F. C. Burkitt of Cambridge, Rev. George Margoliouth of the British Museum, and Dr. M. Gaster. To my colleague, at University College, Professor W. P. Ker, my warm thanks are hereby rendered for his generous offer to defray the extra cost of the illustrations; and I am further pleased gratefully to acknowledge my indebtedness to two other kind friends, interested in literature generally, for the practical help which they have accorded me.

H. G.

TRANSLATION. CODEX A

§ 1. By the Divine power, the servant, the sinner, begins to write the 'Book of Protection'.

First, the anathema by the prayer[1]: Our Father which art in heaven, hallowed be thy name. Thy Kingdom come, and thy will be done, as in heaven, so on earth. Give us the bread which we need for the day. Forgive us our trespasses and sins, as we also forgive those who sin against us. And lead us not into temptation, but deliver us from evil: for Thine is the Kingdom, the power, and the glory, for ever and ever.

§ 2. The Prayer of Adam.

We acknowledge thee, O Lord of All: and thee, O Jesus Christ, we glorify, for thou art the reviver of our bodies, and the redeemer of our souls.

§ 3. The Prayer of the Holy Angels.

O holy God, holy Mighty One, holy Immortal: O our Lord, have pity upon us: O our Lord, receive thou our petition: O our Lord, be gracious unto this thy servant who bears these writs[2]. Amen! Amen!

---

[1] Matt. vi. 9-13; Luke xi. 2-4.

[2] A magical scrap of writing or talisman is called ܪ̈ܳܩܶܐ (only in plural in this sense). *Cf.* Matt. v. 18, where sing. occurs with the meaning 'jot'; the word 'tittle' is rendered by ܣܪܝܛܐ (lit. 'scratch', sc. of pen), an expression which frequently occurs at the end of a work ܐܬܟܬܒ ܣܪܝܛ this book has been 'scratched' and 'written'. In modern language one still says: ܟܬܘܒ ܠܝ ܚܕ ܐܘ ܬܪܝܢ ܣܪ̈ܛܝܢ 'Write me one or two lines or words'.

§ 4. The Anathema of the Gospel, which is of avail for all pains and all sicknesses.

In the beginning was the Word: that Word was with God. And this Word was God, and the same was in the beginning with God. And all was by his hand, and without him there was not one thing (made) of that which was. In him was life, and the life was the light of men. That light is in the darkness: it preventeth it not. By the power of those Ten Words, proceeding from the Lord God, and by the name I Am That I Am, Almighty God, Adonai, Lord of Hosts, may there be distanced and destroyed all the evil and abominable actions of accursed demons, and all their practices, and all opposition, temptations, unclean spirits, and stumbling-blocks, sounds, and creakings, fear and trembling that come to oppose, devices, malice, and evil occurrences, also the effects and bonds of witchcraft, the hot and cold fever, the fever-horror, and the Jewish (fever), [may they be driven] from the body and soul of the one who bears these writs, by the prayer of my Lady, the blessed Mary, and of Mar John the Baptist. Amen!

§ 5. The Anathema of Mar George, which is of avail for fear and trembling.

In the name of the Father, the Son, and the Holy Ghost. The prayer, request, petition, and supplication of Mar George, the glorious martyr, which he prayed before God, saying:—O Lord, God of Hosts, grant me this request: May the twofold danger be annulled from off the flocks, from the cattle, and from the house of him who beareth these writs. Furthermore, may there be bound the inflammation, the pestilence, and jaundice (?)[1], the sickness of Moṣul, by

---

[1] I have here rendered the word ꙮꙮ 'jaundice' as an abbreviation of ꙮꙮ. In A, § 26, it seems to be the name of a place known for a certain sickness. The name occurs as that of a town in Egypt, and a similarly sounding name is found on the frontier between Persia and

the prayers of Abba Mark and by the supplication of Abba Pahum : may there be bound and expelled the twofold dangers from the flocks and from the cattle of him who beareth these writs, by the command of the Messiah, the Redeemer of the world, and by that prayer which our Lord prayed when they crucified him in Jerusalem, and by the name I Am That I Am, Almighty God, Adonai, Lord of Hosts, by the prayers of Abba Pahum, which he prayed, and the pestilence was stayed ; [so may these evils be chased] from off the flocks and the cattle of the one who beareth these writs ; the merit was reckoned unto him for all generations and for evermore, by the prayers of my Lady, the blessed Mary, and of Mar John the Baptist. Amen !

§ 6. [PRAYER WHICH IS OF AVAIL] BEFORE THE AUTHORITIES.

In the name of the Father, the Son, and the Holy Ghost. I take hold of the Father in secret, and openly I am wrapped with the Son, and mysteriously doth the Holy Spirit dwell within me ; verily I fear no evil. As regards every one who dares to look at the bearer of these writs, I bind and curse him by the Word which our Lord addressed unto his disciples : ' Whatsoever ye shall bind on earth, shall be bound in heaven.' Thus, O Lord, God of Hosts, I bind the mouths and tongues of all wicked persons, thieves, robbers, and highwaymen, men of power, men in authority, and men of violence, prefects, ...[1] and chiefs from off the one who beareth these writs ; [I bind them] by the power and the garment with which Alexander, the son of Philip, was clothed, with which he subdued the whole earth ; thus, O Lord, God of

Afghanistan. Is it perhaps an abbreviated form (the first syllable) of 'Constantinople' ܩܘܣܛܢܛܝܢܘܦܘܠܝܣ ?

[1] The word ܢܣܘܕܐ between 'prefects' and 'chiefs' I have left untranslated. It may be an error for ܩܫܝܐ 'harsh', 'violent ones', or ܩܢܝܐ 'jealous ones'.

Hosts, may the head of all wicked persons be humbled before the one who beareth these writs by the sword of the Synod and by the stones of Philon[1]. O Lord, God of Hosts, as thou didst cause Joseph to go forth from the prison-house, and didst preserve Moses from the hands of King Pharaoh, and didst deliver David from Saul, and didst save Elijah from Ahab, and those of the house of Hananiah from the fiery furnace, and Daniel from the Babylonians, so, I beseech thee, O Lord, God of Hosts, that this thy servant who beareth these writs may have an open and winning countenance before kings, men in authority, men of violence, chiefs and captains of the host, as had Peter, Paul, and Gabriel. In like manner, O Lord, God of Hosts, as thou didst rejoice thy disciples in the city Cana[2], so rejoice thou this thy servant who beareth these [writs] before kings and the authorities, that the mouths and tongues of evil persons be bound away from him. So be it, Amen!

§ 7. [PRAYER WHICH IS OF AVAIL] BEFORE THE AUTHORITIES.

In the name of the Father, the Son, and the Holy Ghost. I mount the lion and the young dragon. Save us, O Lord, from the man of wickedness by the word and commandment of our Lord, Jesus Christ, who overthrew kings (depriving them) of their crowns, and chiefs, magistrates, rulers and governors (depriving them) of their thrones. By that power which was with Joseph in the land of Egypt, may the beauty of the one who beareth these writs shine before kings and rulers, as the sun in the days of Nisan, and as the moon in

---

[1] I shall be glad to have some light thrown upon the meaning of this latter clause. I was once informed by a native of Mesopotamia that the front of the dress of the priests of Chaldea is adorned with 'stones'. But is the robe itself called Pylon or Philon? Or, does 'the Synod' suggest the Greek 'Council' called *Pylaea*, Πυλαία, for ܦܝܠܐ ?

[2] John ii. 1–11.

the nights of Ellul, and as the garden in the hands of the gardener. By the prayers of the just and righteous ones do I bind the tongues of evil men, men of power and violent, judges, and chiefs, from off the one who beareth these formulae, Gabriel (being) on his right and Michael on his left, I Am That I Am, Almighty God, Adonai (being) above his head, the Cherubim in front of him, and the Seraphim behind him: nor will he fear the man of wickedness. In all the earth may there light upon him compassion and mercy, and may they favour him from near, and worship him from afar, may he hold the sword in his right hand, and the bow in his left, so that his head may be exalted before kings, rulers, prefects, judges, and chiefs, and he will rule over him [1]. As the beauty of Moses shone upon the children of Israel, so may the beauty of him who carrieth (these) writs shine forth before kings, rulers, commanders, and chiefs. As the crown of Pharaoh before Joseph, so may there bow down to him the rich and the poor, the base and the wicked ones, the men of power and force, [departing] from him who beareth these amulets, by the prayer of my Lady, the blessed Mary. Amen!

§ 8. FOR A MAN GOING TO LAW.

In the name of the Father, the Son, and the Holy Ghost, Patre et Filio et Spiritu Sancto, let him go forth—not by himself alone—to judgment and victory [2]. So may the angel Gabriel be on my right, the Cherubim on my left, and hovering over me and protecting me be the name I Am That I Am, Almighty God, Adonai, Lord of Hosts: may the mighty I AM, and He majestic in holiness be above my head, and protect me from all the enemies of my name, and humble all those who would lift themselves against me from above, from below, from before me and from behind (lit. those who sit before me and those round about me). May they (God's

---

[1] Rule over 'the man of wickedness'.　　　　[2] *Cf.* Matt. xii. 20.

names) be a helper, a redeemer, and protector unto me, that
they may receive me as a chalice, and place me on their heads
as a crown, in the name of Christ, the King, who judges all
mine enemies. From now unto thee, O Holy One, our Father
in Heaven, [I pray] be thou with me, come to my aid, and
redeem me: and may the four Evangelists come to my help,
Matthew, Mark, Luke, and John. By the prayers of these
holy ones [and by the prayer of] my Lady, the blessed Mary,
may they (God's names) be with him who beareth these writs.
So be it, Amen!

§ 9. BINDING THE ARROWS, DAGGERS, SWORDS, AND ALL IMPLEMENTS OF WAR.

In the name of the Father, the Son, and the Holy Ghost.
By the crucifixion on the Cross, when our Lord cried out upon
the Cross, and said: 'My God, my God, why hast thou
forsaken me?'[1] the earth trembled at his splendour, and
the heavens at his glory: by that great and terrible name,
and that exalted and mighty arm, I bind, anathematize, and
expel from off him who beareth these writs the arrows, bows,
swords, and knives,—all the implements of war belonging to
wicked men: [according to the words] 'He (God) maketh
wars to cease unto the end of the earth; he breaketh the
bows, and cutteth the spears in sunder; he burneth the
chariots in the fire'[2]. 'Their sword shall enter into their
own heart: as for his arrows, the Lord hath scattered them'[3].
May they (these war instruments) be bound by me by means
of those seven priests who advance and retire, without be-
holding the countenance of their Lord: may they be bound
by me through Elijah, the prophet, son of Eliezer the priest,
who bound the heavens for three years and six months, so that
no rain came down upon the earth. By all these names

[1] Ps. xxii. 1; Matt. xxvii. 46; Mark xv. 34. [2] Ps. xlvi. 9.
[3] Ps. xxxvii. 15; only former half agrees.

I bind their arrows, in fine, all the war-implements of enemies. ' He ordaineth their arrows against the persecutors : because he travaileth with iniquity and hath conceived false-hood, and brought forth oppression ' [1]. May they be bound by me beneath the throne of the Living God, and by means of Him who sitteth upon it. ' And thou shalt not be afraid of the terror of the night : nor for the arrow that flieth by day ' [2]. As far as the east is from the west, and the north from the south, so may there be far removed and destroyed from off the one who beareth these writs, the arrows, swords, daggers, and guns of wicked men, thieves, and robbers, by the prayer of my Lady, the blessed Mary. Amen !

§ 10. THE ANATHEMA OF KING SOLOMON, WHICH IS OF AVAIL FOR AN INJURY (?) TO THE BACK [3].

In the name of the Father, the Son, and the Holy Ghost : and in the name of I Am That I Am, Almighty God, Adonai, Lord of Hosts. King Solomon was building the House to the name of the Lord, and the Holy Spirit was handing him the stone : Solomon stooped to take hold of the stone : he hurt (?) his back, his loin ruptured, and he gave forth a bitter cry. Whereupon our Lord said unto his disciples : What voice of crying is this ? and they replied unto him : It is that of Solomon, the son of David, who is building the terrific, blessed House. Amen !

§ 11. FOR EVERY SICKNESS.

In the name of the Father, the Son, and the Holy Ghost. By thy great and fearful name, and by the power of thy help, O Living King, full of compassion, rich in gifts, and abounding in love, I stretch forth my hand and call unto thee, O our Lord, Jesus Christ, and upon thy Holy Name,

---

[1] Ps. vii. 13, 14 ; Scripture has ' his (God's) arrows ', here ' their own '.
[2] Ps. xci. 5.   [3] Perhaps ' lumbago '.

which thou hast put upon the dead and they came to life, and the leprous became cleansed, and the blind had their eyes opened, and those sick of the palsy thou didst heal in thy grace: (concerning) the fever-horror, fear, and trembling, the head-ache, eyes-ache, and every pain and grievous sickness, which lay hold of mankind, as thy command chased the fever-horror from the mother-in-law of Simon Peter, and caused the light of righteousness to shine upon that man, out of whom six devils went forth: and thou didst heal them in thy grace, namely, her from whom the blood flowed, and thou didst make whole the man sick of the palsy by the living word proceeding from thy lips: and by thy living and holy voice didst thou rebuke the sea, which was by the lake Tiberias, and didst calm the billows and the tempests in the sea, and there was a great calm and rest[1], so now, we beseech thee, grant strength to the weak, and send thy help unto this thy servant who beareth these writs. May he be healed from all pains and sicknesses and grievous sufferings by the prayer of all the saints. Amen!

§ 12. THE ANATHEMA OF MAR THOMAS[2], WHICH IS OF AVAIL FOR THE SPIRIT OF LUNACY.

In the name of the Father, the Son, and the Holy Ghost. The prayer, request, petition, and supplication of Mar George (*sic*), the glorious martyr, who lived in the mountain for forty years. He was torn as rags[3], and blood flowed from them (i. e. the rents made in his flesh): and he prayed and said, 'O Lord, God of Hosts, I beseech thee, and supplicate thy grace, and ask the same request which Peter, Paul, and Gabriel—chief of the angels, besought on account of the evil spirit of lunacy. I bind you away from the three hundred

---

[1] *Cf.* Matt. viii and ix.

[2] In the heading we have Mar Thomas, whilst in the body of the charm Mar George is named.

[3] Or 'into rags': *cf.* Isa. lxiv. 6.

and sixty-six members of the one who carrieth these writs:
and you are bound by me, O evil Spirit of Lunacy, and you
have not the power to reside in the body and soul of the one
who carrieth these writs, but you will needs go forth from
the bones, from the sinews, from the flesh, from the skin,
and from the hair unto the ground, and from the ground
(passing on) to iron, and from iron to stone, and from stone
(you will pass on) to the mountain. This writing must be
sealed. Amen, Amen!

§ 13. FOR PAIN IN THE HEAD.

In the name of the Father, the Son, and the Holy Ghost.
By thy name, O God,—the hope of all who are bound and op-
pressed, we bind and anathematize, expel and destroy and drive
out, the pains and all the maladies which reside in the head,
in the eyes, and in the ears, which are in number seventy-two
aches: and these are the names by which they are called,
evil spirits, red maladies[1], black maladies, harsh and sweet
sounds. We bind, anathematize, and drive out, and thrust
away these evil spirits from the head, and from the eyes, and
from the temples, and from the cheeks, and from all the
members of the person who beareth these writs. By the
name of the Word of the Lord, in whose dominion are the
heaven and the earth, and at whom the rebellious demons
tremble: by the name I Am That I Am, Almighty God,
Adonai, Lord of Hosts, and by the name Gannus and Sloonus,
men of fire, and by the name Gabriel and Michael, by the
prayers of Mar Simon Peter, we bind and anathematize all
evil aches from the head, and from the eyes, and from the
eyebrows, and from the temples, and from the cheeks, and
from all the members of the person who carries these formulae.
Amen!

---

[1] Lit. 'noises', 'creakings'.

e

§ 14. FOR THE LOOSENING (OF OBJECTS) OF THE CHASE.

In the name of the Father, the Son, and the Holy Ghost. As Simon Peter and Andrew threw the nets[1], (and had) a goodly and abundant catch of large fish, so do I loosen the (objects of) chase for the one who carries these writs, for his dog, and for his company, and for the mountains in which they go. I loosen them by the Living God, who loosens them in heaven; as God loosened Joseph from the slavery of Egypt, so do I loosen the (objects of) chase on behalf of A., the son of B.[2]

In the name of the Father, the Son, and the Holy Ghost. The Lord looked from heaven upon the earth: and in order to loosen the (objects of) chase from the rest, and mankind from death, sent down to them flesh like the dust, and like the sand of the seas the winged fowl of heaven, so that the righteous ones might grow strong in glory. Thus may the chase come from the East and from the West, and from the four corners of the world: may it come and enter into his (the huntsman's) hands, and in front of the gun of A., the son of B. Amen!

§ 15. FOR THE RICHES (OR SUSTENANCE) OF MAN.

In the name of the Father, the Son, and the Holy Ghost. By thy name, Lord of the Universe and of Creatures, we pray thee, O Lord, God of Hosts, (God) of every breathing thing that exists in heaven and on earth, Creator of Adam and his Hope, who breathed within him the spirit and he lived, and gave him dominion over all things, who said unto Noah, 'Make unto thee an ark of wood, and gather within it every creeping thing, bird, and fowl of heaven'[3]; thus, by the command of the Living God, may (all things) be gathered and enter into the house of him who beareth these writs, and

---

[1] Matt. iv. 18; Luke v.

[2] Lit. So-and-so, the son of So-and-so.   [3] Gen. vii.

may they benefit him (as) a good fortune, and may all the advantages and good and fine provisions from heaven and from earth come in great quantity from all men, bearing the good things and coming to the house of him who carries (these) writs, and to the places in which this writing will be (hung), may they come. All those who behold him will come, bearing and presenting gifts to him who carries these writings, in the name of those angels who came to the house of Abraham, and blessed him, and increased the riches of his house; so, by the command of God, in their name, may everything be blessed which is, and which will be unto him who beareth these writs. Amen!

§ 16. BINDING THE GUNS AND THE ENGINE OF WAR.

In the name of the Father, the Son, and the Holy Ghost. The voice of our Lord which cutteth the flame of the fire [1]: the voice of the Lord against Gog and Magog, the governors and chiefs of Meshech and Togarmah [2]: the voice of the Lord against the craft of wicked enemies, against evil-doers, and against the stones which they fling with the machine and with the gun. May these (stones) not be moved, nor heated, nor come forth from their (machines' or guns') mouths against the one who beareth these writs, but let them be as the dead in the midst of the grave. Amen!

‘O thou, Capernaum, which art exalted unto heaven, shalt be brought down to hell!’ [3]

‘And when Jesus was entered into the ship, and his disciples followed him, and they awoke him, saying unto him, Save us, Lord, for lo we perish! Then Jesus arose, and rebuked the sea’ [4]. By that power I bind, expel, anathematize the bullets (lit. stones) of the engines of war, and the balls of the guns of the wicked enemies away from him who beareth these writs,

---

[1] Ps. xxix. 7.   [2] Ezek. xxxviii. 2, 3, 6; xxvii. 13, 14.

[3] Matt. xi. 23; Luke x. 15.

[4] *Cf.* Matt. viii. 23-26; Mark iv. 37-39; Luke viii. 22-24.

by the prayer of the Holy Virgin, the Mother of Fire[1].
Amen!

§ 17. FOR CHATTERING TEETH.

GMIHID, GIHID, GHTR, GMHTR. Write (these
words) upon the wood of a twig[2], and hang (it) in the house.

Another (formula) for the teeth[3] and for the molars.

As for me Jacob cut-in-pieces[4], when the time arrived for
me to be martyred by the persecutors, and the executioners
were surrounding me, clutching their sharpened swords, I
said: I beg of you, leave me alone until I have prayed.
And when they gave me permission, I moved aside somewhat,
and thus did I speak: O Lord, I beg of Thee, as regards all
who make mention of thy holy Name, Our Lord, Jesus
Christ, and of my name, thy servant Jacob, and will write
and hang (the formula) on their person, that the pain of the
teeth[5] may no longer be unto him: but I anathematize this
malady, I, Jacob, in the name of the Father, the Son, and
the Holy Ghost. May no pain be unto him who beareth
these formulae, neither as regards his teeth, nor his molars, by
the prayers of my Lady, the blessed Mary. Amen!

§ 18. CONCERNING THE PEACE OF MEN, ONE WITH
THE OTHER.

In the name (of the Father[6]), the Son, and the Holy Ghost.

In the name of our Lord Jesus Christ, the Peace of the
world, grant peace unto thy servants one with the other
towards him who beareth these writs, by that Voice (Bath-

---

[1] This expression occurs in the prayers and benedictions of the Chaldeans at the present day.

[2] ܚܠܦܐ (Ḥĕlāpā), modern Syriac for ܥܪܒܬܐ ' willow-tree '.

[3] ܟܟܐ Neo-Syriac.

[4] *Vide* Castelli, *Lexicon Syr.*, p. 717, citing Assemani A. m. O.

[5] I have rendered the two terms by ' teeth '.

[6] Omitted in MS.; to be supplied.

Kol) [1] which called unto Cain, the murderer, 'Where is thy brother, Abel?' and he boldly replied to it, 'Am I my brother's keeper?' [2] He is thy friend' [3]. In like manner may there be cut off wily action, and may there too be annulled from the house of him who beareth these writs, jealousy and enmity, disputes, strifes, and divisions; by that Word which spake to the water and it became wine [4], may (men) be at peace with one another, may the gates of mercy and compassion be opened, and the mouth of evil men be stopped from off him; yea may his mouth be closed and stopped, that they shall not again be able to dispute with one another, but that they shall be at peace and harmony by the name of the glorified Trinity, the Father, the Son, and the Holy Ghost. Amen!

§ 19. CONCERNING . . . . [5]

Pronounce the blessing over barley and corn. In the name of the Father, the Son, and the Holy Ghost. Boil it and bring it . . . [6] through the merit of Esau [7], of Moses, of

---

[1] On this curious expression see Dr. Edwin A. Abbott's *From Letter to Spirit*, which contains in Appendix IV an interesting and exhaustive explanation.

[2] Gen. iv. 9.   [3] A strange interpolation.   [4] John ii. 1-11.

[5] I had at first intended to dismiss this tantalizing passage, and leave it untranslated, as Arabic gibberish, or rather an admixture of Syriac, Arabic, and other forms. But after a deal of thought and investigation, I have attempted, subject to future revision, some sort of translation of almost the whole section. The rendering of the latter portion is conjectural. The one-word heading is a great stumbling-block. From its form one would take it to be Persian or Turkish, but I can find no satisfactory explanation. The ܕ is undoubtedly the preposition 'concerning'. Is the word, perhaps, after all, a transposed plural form of the Syriac ܟܘ̈ܒܝܬܐ 'spider'?

[6] ܗܡܫܗܪܝ, *ham-shahri* in Persian means 'townsman'.

[7] The British Museum Codex (B. M.) has ܕܡܘܣܝܣ, which is certainly better.

David[1], of Solomon, of Gabriel, the great Angel[2], peace be upon him ! With a loud voice throw[3] with sixty-six[4] ounces (?)[5] towards the sky[6], each ounce (?)[7] . . . .[8]. Crush frankincense, cry (?)[9] BLN, BLN, CLN, CLN. Break upon them (the sounds) BIGU, BIGU, BIGANA[10], JRJI, JRJI, JRJANA[11], from a grunting reed—a clear, swelling torrent[12], drawing out the trumpet-sound (?)[13] of effective extermination[14] from off him who bears this charm, Amen !

§ 20. CONCERNING CRAMP[15] AT THE HEART.

Say the benediction over butter, and give him to drink (of it). In the name of the Father, the Son, and the Holy Ghost. Our Lord and his disciples were walking on the way, and they heard the sound of an exclamation, and our Lord said : What sound is this ? They replied unto him, It is that of one who bears these writs, having been seized by a cramp

---

[1] Note the Arabic forms in ܪܝܡܐ (for ܪܡܐ), ܕܐܘܕ, ܣܘܠܝܡܢ.

[2] Arabic ܐܠܡܠܟ; Arabic ܐܠܡܠܐܟ, with the ܘ omitted before ܝ.

[3] I cannot deal with the ܢܢ before ܪܡܝ (cf. Appendix, B. M.).

[4] The ܩ or ܣ in ܣܬܝܢ ܘܫܬ (Arabic forms) is evidently a scribe's error.

[5] ܐܘܢܩܐ. Is it ܐܘܢܩܝܐ 'uncia'?

[6] I take it to be the Persian *āsmān*, 'heaven', 'the celestial orb'.

[7] Undoubtedly the same as ܐܘܢܩܐ.

[8] I will not venture upon a rendering of these five words.

[9] I take ܩܪܝ to be ܩܪܝ.

[10] We have in Persian *bīgāh*, 'ill-timed'; *bīgānah*, 'alien', 'stranger'; and *bijān*, 'lifeless'.

[11] *Jarjar* in Persian is 'a camel braying'; *jarjarat*, 'the noise of a camel braying'.

[12] *Tartār*, Persian for 'a raging, swelling torrent'.

[13] The MS. may read ܐܠܛܒܐ: is it, therefore, a compound of the Arabic 'Al' and the Aramaic ܛܒܛ 'trumpet-blast'?

[14] From ܣܘ, an irregular form.

[15] *See* Introduction.

(rheumatism) in his heart and in all his members. I said[1]:
(as a remedy) for teeth (which have fallen) from the mouth,
and for a child (which has fallen) from its mother, Go to the
garden of our Lord, and cut three branches, one in the name
of our Lord Jesus Christ, the second in the name of our
Lady, the blessed Mary, and the other in the name of Gabriel
chief of the angels, and smite the spirit in the heart of the
one who carries these writs, by the prayer of the blessed
Mar Augin (Eugenius)[2]. Amen!

§ 21. BINDING THE MOUTH OF DOGS.

In the name of the Father, the Son, and the Holy Ghost.
'By the greatness of thine arm they shall sink as stones'[3].
Make them still, O Lord God, make them still by that stone
which was put upon the mouth of the tomb of our Redeemer.
By it may these dogs be silenced through the prayers of my
Lady, the blessed Mary, and of Mar John the Baptist, and
through the prayer of all the martyrs and saints of our
Lord. Amen!

Say the benediction over three morsels, and throw them in
front of the dogs[4].

§ 22. BINDING THE EVIL APPARITION.

In the name of the Father, the Son, and the Holy Ghost.
My brother Moses—the servant of God—was tending the
sheep between seven mountains[5], and there met him three
evil forms: one was an evil man, (the other) an evil wolf,
and (the third) an evil lion.

[1] Perhaps: 'I have remarked in another work, &c.' Or, 'As I once
remarked in the case of teeth, &c.', so I now say, 'Go to the garden of
our Lord, &c.'

[2] Occurs in Rabbinic literature as an attribute, 'noble born', not as
a proper name. [3] Cf. Exod. xv. 16.

[4] This ought, in all probability, to come at the beginning of § 21; cf. § 20.

[5] The Bible makes no mention of *seven* mountains; the author is, perhaps,
thinking of the *seven* hills of Rome, or using the round number *seven*.

In the name of the Father, may the evil man be bound by
me; in the name of the Son, may the evil wolf be bound by
me; in the name of the Holy Ghost, may the evil lion be
bound by me, so that they may not approach the person, nor
the house of him who beareth these writs, through the prayer
of the Virgin Mary. Amen!

§ 23. THE ANATHEMA OF THE ANGEL GABRIEL, WHICH IS
OF AVAIL FOR THE EVIL EYE.

In the name of the Father, the Son, and the Holy Ghost.
The Evil Eye went forth from the stone of the rock, and
the angel Gabriel met her. He said unto her: Whither
goest thou, O daughter of destruction? She replied unto
him, I am going to destroy men and women, boys and girls,
the souls of cattle, and the fowl of heaven. The angel
Gabriel said unto her : Hast thou not been to Paradise, and
seen the Great God, the One who is surrounded by thousands
upon thousands and myriads upon myriads of angels, who
sanctify him? By His name thou art bound by me, and
I bind thee, O Evil and Envious Eye, and Eye of seven evil
neighbours! It is not within thy power to approach either
the body or the soul, or the spirit, or the connexions of the
sinews, or the 366 members[1] which are in the frame of the
one who carries these formulae, through the prayer of my
Lady, the blessed Mary, and of Mar John the Baptist.
Amen!

§ 24. FOR THE COW WHICH DISLIKES, OR IS EXCITED
TOWARDS, HER MISTRESS[2].

In the name of the Father, the Son, and the Holy Ghost.
We beg of Thee, O Lord, God of Hosts, that by thy exalted

---

[1] So also § 12. *Cf.* the Rabbinic conception (as in Targum Jer. on Gen.
i. 27), that the human body consists of 248 members and 365 nerves,
corresponding respectively to the number of affirmative and prohibitive
precepts in the Torah, which together make up the total 613.

[2] The position of ܐܪ and the endings ܢ are peculiar.

and strong arm, this beast may be fond of and subject herself to her mistress and her son. Guard her against the evil and envious eye, by the power of thy beloved Son, our Lord Jesus Christ, and by the power of the angels who minister before Thee both night and day, who exclaim and repeat, 'Holy, Holy, Holy is the Lord God of Hosts, the heaven and the earth are full of his glory!' [1] Make this cow at peace with her mistress A. the daughter of B., so that she may milk her by thy living and holy command, by the sanctification of those on high, and the action of those below, through the prayer of my Lady, the blessed Mary, and Mar John the Baptist. Amen!

§ 25. BINDING THE COLIC AND THE COLD.

In the name of the Father, the Son, and the Holy Ghost. (The effects) of cold are groaning and brooding, killing even giants, to which our Lord, as a little boy, and his mother were subject [2]. In the name of our Lord, may the cold and the colic be expelled and extirpated from one side and from two sides, from the right side and from the left side of him who bears these writs. Amen!

§ 26. FOR THE PESTILENCE AMONG SHEEP AND LARGER ANIMALS.

In the name of the Father, the Son, and the Holy Ghost. Our Lord went to the Mountain of Sinai, and saw the sheep of Abraham which Satan had killed, and he told one of the angels to protect and help (whatever he saw) of all that vision. May no hateful visitation approach either the cattle, or the sheep, or whatever there is, or there will be belonging unto the one who bears these writings, neither by night, nor by day, nor at even-tide, nor in the morning, nor at noon-

---

[1] *Cf.* Isa. vi. 6.

[2] At the time of his birth, always represented in winter time. If this be the meaning, it is badly put in the original.

time, nor sleeping nor rising. May the pestilence be annulled from off the sheep and the cattle of the one who beareth these writs. May no malady or sickness of Kūs [1], or sickness of Mosul, or evil and envious eye, or the wily eye of wicked men (approach him) [2] : but may evil demons and (their) cursed practices be removed from the sheep of the servant of Christ, A., the son of B. Amen!

§ 27. THE ANATHEMA OF RABBAN HURMIZD, WHICH IS OF AVAIL FOR MAD DOGS.

In the name of the Father, the Son, and the Holy Ghost. The prayer, request, petition, and supplication of Mar Rabban Hurmizd of Persia, son of Joseph the Chief, which he prayed and asked of the Merciful and Compassionate God at the time of his martyrdom. He said: O Lord, God of Hosts, I beg of Thee, and supplicate thy Grace, that (as regards) every one who will make mention of thy Holy Name, and of my name—thy servant Hurmizd of the Persians [3], may the mad dog neither bite nor put his teeth in him : but let the destructive lion, the daring tiger, the pig, and the lurking wolf, and all dangerous animals (be kept aloof [4]) from him and from his house, from his sons and daughters, and from all that there is and will be unto him who beareth these writings, through the prayer of my Lady, the blessed Mary. Amen!

§ 28. BINDING THE FEVER.

In the name of the Father, the Son, and the Holy Ghost. Christ suffered, Christ was crucified, Christ died, Christ rose. May there be cut off and expelled from the body and soul of A., the son of B., the hot and cold fever, the fever-horror, and the Jewish (fever) [5], in fine, all sorts of fever. As far as the

[1] *Cf.* § 5, where I have translated 'jaundice—the sickness of Mosul .
[2] It seems necessary to supply this.
[3] The original is Agami, old name for Persians.
[4] Has to be supplied.   [5] *Cf.* § 4.

East is from the West, and the North is from the South, may there depart and be removed the hot and cold fever, the fever-horror, and all sorts of fever from the body and soul of the one who carries these formulae. So be it, Amen!

§ 29. BENEDICTION FOR VINEYARDS AND CORN-FIELDS.

Pronounce the benediction over the seed :—

In the name of the Father, the Son, and the Holy Ghost. Glory to Thee, O God! Glory to Thee, O Planter of all trees, bearing fine fruit for the enjoyment of his servants. Bless, O my Lord, the seed and all the crops of the one who beareth these writs, also his vineyard, whatever he hath, and whatever he will have, that they may be covered with joyous fruits. Remove from them the evil and envious eye; and may drought and hard growth, hail and locust, and the worm, and all plagues, be annulled from off his seed, his vineyard, his crops, his field, and from all that he hath, and will have, namely, the one who beareth these writs. Amen!

§ 30. FOR RECONCILIATION IN THE HOUSEHOLD.

In the name of the Father, the Son, and the Holy Ghost. Christ, the Peace of those above, and the great Rest of those below! O my Lord, suffer thy peace to dwell among this household of those who worship Thee: may they be in peace and harmony with each other; as the line in the soil is to the husbandman, as the servant is to the master, and as the maid is to the mistress, so may the members of the household of the one who bears these writs be rendered subservient, through the prayer of all the martyrs and saints of our Lord. Amen!

§ 31. FOR THE JOURNEY AND FOR MERCHANDISE, THAT IS, ON BUSINESS.

In the name of the Father, the Son, and the Holy Ghost. The Power which compelled into the Ark of Noah all creeping things, birds, and fowl, *et cetera*, may He gather

large and fine and marvellous fortunes (lit. wedges) unto the house of the one who beareth these writs. May the letter (of business) proceed empty from his house, and may it return laden (with orders): and may his business rise in the proportion of thirty, sixty, or even one hundred to one. May his journey be guarded against all evil enemies, and may the Lord help and support him against all losses on his way; may the house of the one who carries these writings be blessed in heaven and on earth, through the prayer of Mar Isaiah of Haleb (Aleppo). Amen!

§ 32. For a man going by night on the way, so that he need not be afraid.

In the name of the Father, the Son, and the Holy Ghost. O God of Abraham, Isaac, and Israel! O God of our Fathers, just and righteous ones! O God, Father of our Lord Jesus Christ, we beseech Thee, and supplicate thy Greatness for the hour on which the one who bears these charms sets out on the way; may thy care accompany him, thou preserving his body and soul from all dangers, and delivering him from all obstacles. As thou wast with Joseph in the land of Egypt, and with Daniel in the lions' den, and with those of the house of Hananiah in the fiery furnace, and with Jeremiah in the pit of mire, so be thou with this thy servant who bears these writs: lighten off from him the tedium of the journey on which he sets out and is taking: cause him to abound with a good result, being (his) support and redeemer. Grant him a winning countenance in the sight of all men: and as regards the land whither he goes, suffer him, O my Lord, to return with his mouth full of thanksgiving, and his tongue full of praise: so that he may return to his house in joy and gladness, and send up to thee praise and glory, and to thy glorious Name thanksgiving and adoration, (O thou, who art) the Protector of thy servants, and the Helper of those who fear Him. Amen!

§ 33. For noises and sounds.

In the name of the Father, the Son, and the Holy Ghost.
By thy name, O God, the Hope of all those who are bound,
I bind the Satan and hindrance (lit. dispute) to the handi-
work of man; and further the sweet and harsh sounds which
cling to the temples corresponding to the eyes of him who
beareth these charms. I bind them away from his head,
from his eyes, from his cheeks, and from the brain of his
head: and it is not in your power to beat or to revolve in the
head or in any of the members of the one who bears this
charm, through the prayer of my Lady, the blessed Mary,
and of Mar John the Baptist, and of Mar Abraham Senior, and
of Mar Abraham Kidunaya, and of Mar Simon bar Sabai.
Amen!

§ 34. For the advantage of the house.

In the name of the Father, the Son, and the Holy Ghost.
May He who satisfied a thousand in the desert, when they
ate of a little bread [1], bless this table, that it may be full
and rich, so that the poor may eat and be satisfied, and the
orphans be fed from it [2]. May all the crowds be seated
around it as (around) the table of Abraham, the Chosen [3];
[and as he was blessed, and as were blessed] David, both
king and prophet, Solomon and Hezekiah, Daniel and Josiah,
and Constantine the Just [4], so, my Lord, may be blessed this
house, that is, that of thy servant, and may it abound in all
good things. O my Lord, bless those who keep it in good
order: bless, O our Lord, those who work in it: bless, O my
Lord, his house: bless, O our Lord, those who dwell therein.
O our Lord, shield his house, and cause to dwell therein the
blessings (wherewith) He blessed the righteous and the

---

[1] *Cf.* Matt. xiv and xv; Mark vi and viii; Luke ix; John vi.

[2] This whole section is rhymed in the original; at all events it has
a rhythmic ring about it.

[3] Abraham, always regarded as the type of hospitality to strangers.

[4] ܟ̈ܢܐ 'meritorious', 'victorious , 'holy', 'pure', often 'Christian'.

fathers[1], the workers of miracles and signs. May his table
be blessed, and his wealth be increased: may his dead ones
rise, may their sins and faults be atoned: [may he be blessed]
now and for all time, for ever and ever. Amen!

§ 35. BINDING THE MOUTH OF WOLVES FROM OFF THE SHEEP AND LARGER ANIMALS.

In the name of the Father, the Son, and the Holy Ghost.
The prayer, request, petition, and supplication[2] of Mar Daniel
the prophet, when he went down into the den of hungry
lions, and they did him no harm[3]. May there be bound,
sealed, and bridled the mouths of wolves, bears, and lions,
the mouth of every destructive animal, from off everything
that there is and will be to the one who bears this charm, by
the staff of Moses the prophet, and by the ring of Solomon
Bar Jaki[4],—from off the cattle and the sheep of A., the son of
B. Furthermore, may there be bound, sealed, and bridled
their mouths and their tongues, so that if it be open it may
not bend it to, and if it be bent it shall not open; by the
prayers of Rabban Hurmizd, and by the request of Mar Elias,
and by the supplication of Mar Daniel the prophet, may the
mouth of wolves, bears, and all (destructive) animals be bound.
Amen!

Pronounce the benediction over the Knife[5].

[1] Should perhaps be ' the righteous fathers'.

[2] ܐܠܘܬܐ is the general term for prayer expressed by the mouth;
ܒܥܘܬܐ prayer by word of mouth accompanied by signs with the
hand; ܣܓܕܬܐ worship by prostrating oneself, with hands and face
on the ground; ܒܪܘܟܬܐ the act of kneeling on the ground and
opening the arms in heartfelt prayer.

[3] Dan. vi. 17 sqq.　　　[4] *Vide* Introduction.

[5] This may belong to the next section or to the present one, coming,
of course, at the beginning: or, it may be the introduction of another
incantation which the writer omits to give.

§ 36. BINDING FALSE DREAMS.

In the name of the Father, the Son, and the Holy Ghost : and by the name I Am That I Am, Almighty God, Adonai, Lord of Hosts; and by the name of Christopher, and by the name of Rabban Hurmizd, and of Mar Pityon, I bind, anathematize, expel and extirpate those evil dreams and all the phantasy of demons that comes at night and by day from wicked demons and from false dreams, [I expel them] from the chambers of the one who carries these writs. As thou didst expel the Legion from the man that dwelt in the tombs [1], so may there be distanced and expelled from the one who bears this charm all [2] evil dreams and startling visions, excitements and anxieties, heaviness and discharge [3], weeping and worrying, dreams evil and false. Amen !

§ 37. BINDING THE SERPENTS.

In the name of the Father, the Son, and the Holy Ghost. As for the crouching lion and the young dragon, I bind their feet, and may they (lit. their soul) enter into the iron chains. As for the poison of the accursed serpent, like that of the deaf adder [that will not hear] the voice of the whisperer, the charmer, and the enchanter [4], May God break their teeth in their mouth [5], and the Lord uproot the serpents' teeth. Thou didst break the heads of the dragons in the water, thou didst crush the heads of the dragons of Leviathan [6], and of all

---

[1] Matt. viii ; Mark v ; Luke viii.

[2] I read ܠܐ for ܡܢ, which latter makes no sense.

[3] I take ܣܘܒܠ = ܡܣܒܐ Lev. xii. 2, 5 ; xv. 19, 20.

[4] *Cf.* Ps. lviii. 4-5. ܢܚܫܝܐ the man who calls the serpent out of the ground ; ܡܒܝܢ the one who gives the people power to touch the serpent without risk of being bitten.

[5] Ps. lviii. 6.   [6] Ps. lxxiv. 13-14.

serpents: of the speckled serpent, the red serpent, the black serpent, and the white serpent, the offspring of deaf serpents.

And the serpent went and adorned herself; she prevented and joined the body of the peacock [1]; she prevented by cunning, which has exercised itself thenceforth and unto all eternity. Amen!

§ 38. BINDING THE SCORPIONS.

Put together the two scorpions: (then say):—Thou art sealed, bridled, and stopped by the two angels Gabriel and Michael. I bind the mouth of the scorpions by the staff of Moses the Prophet, by the mantle of Elisha [2], by the ascent of Elijah, and by the ring of Solomon bar Jaki [3]. Amen!

§ 39. AS REGARDS CATTLE, THAT THE EVIL EYE SHALL NOT TOUCH IT [4].

In the name of the Father, the Son, and the Holy Ghost. [I said] to the seven accursed brothers, sons of the evil and accursed man: 'Whither are you creeping along on your knees, and moving upon your feet, and crawling upon your hands?' The wicked sons of the wicked and accursed man replied: 'We are creeping along on our knees, walking upon our hands, and moving upon our feet, so that we may eat flesh, and drink [blood] in our palms.' And when I saw them,

---

[1] *Vide* Introduction (Weil's *Biblical Legends*—'The Peacock and the Serpent'). It is interesting in this connexion to compare the Rabbinic interpretation of Gen. vi. 7 in the Midrash, *Bereshith Rabba*, § 28 (towards the end):—הכל קלקלו מעשיהן בדור המבול, הכלב היה הולך אצל הזאב, והתרנגול היה מהלך אצל הטווס, וג'.

[2] *Cf.* Codex B, § 5. For ܐܣܟܡܐ see Nöldeke's *Syriac Grammar* (Eng. Edit., p. 58).

[3] *See* Introduction.   [4] *Cf.* Cod. B, § 10.

I cursed them in the name of the Father, the Son, and the
Holy Ghost, which is Eternal, and a third of God: (saying),
' You are accursed and bound in the name of Gabriel, Michael,
and Azrael, the three holy angels; in the name of that angel
who judged the woman that combed (the hair of) her head
on the eve of holy Sunday; and in the name of the Lord
of the angels; so that you may not proceed on your way,
nor finish your journey. May God break your teeth, and cut
the veins of your head, and the nerves [1] of your teeth, (keeping
them off) from the cattle of the one who carries these writs.
As the smoke vanishes from before the wind, may they vanish,
in the name of the Father, the Son, and the Holy Ghost; in
the name of the Father, the Fatherhood, in the name of the
Son, the Lordship, and in the name of the Holy Ghost, the
Emanation: in the name of the glorious Trinity, now, and
for all time, for ever and ever. Amen! '

§ 40. FOR FAVOUR IN THE SIGHT OF ALL MEN.

In the name of the Father, the Son, and the Holy Ghost.
As God loved Solomon, and he subjected the rebellious devils
by his ring [2]; and as God loved Moses, and divided the Red
Sea before him: and as God loved Joseph, and made him, in
place of a servant, lord over all Egypt, so, O Lord, God of
Hosts, cast the flame [fire] of benevolence towards the bearer
of these writs into the heart of rulers, judges, prefects, chiefs,
officers, and commanders. I bind and bridle their mouths
and tongues by the power of Elijah the Prophet, by which he
bound the heavens three years and six months [3], so that no
rain came down upon the earth; and by the name, I Am
That I Am, Almighty God, Adonai, Lord of Hosts. Amen !

[1] ܟ.ܬ.ܝܘ is modern, ܟ.ܝ.ܠ old Syriac for ' nerves ' or ' vein '.
[2] *Vide* § 41.
[3] Luke iv. 25; Jas. v. 17. *Cf.* 1 Kings xvii. 1, xviii. 1.

g

§ 41. The names [1] on the ring of King Solomon, which are of avail before kings.

In the name of the Father, the Son, and the Holy Ghost.

HKU PṢ	PTPNT	LM PṢ	
DHṢT	PṢ D MṢ T	SHHLT	RḤMT
V ḤLIPT	L MṢ TM PṢ	SHCLLT	TURṢF
KPIDT	DM PṢ T	MRIPT	PṢ JT
ḤSPT	SHPLT	CTIBT	PṢ JT
DM PṢ	BRULḤT	HKIKT	
TRCLT PPT	PRISHT	ALILT	
PPISHNT	JSHRIET	PLISHT [2]	

May these names be a support and a precaution and a (means of) redemption and protection against all pains and sicknesses: also now (a precaution) before kings and judges so that there may be a frank countenance to the one who carries this charm. Amen!

§ 42. Binding the sorcerers.

Confound them, Harshael, Gabriel, and Azrael! Silence (lit. 'make dumb') the hearts and thoughts of wicked men, and evil rulers and oppressors, from off the one who bears this charm. In the name of Tumael stop their lips with something bad and horrid (when) with the one who bears this charm, through the prayer of my Lady, the blessed Mary. Amen!

---

[1] *See* Introduction.

[2] In the circle occurring on p. 54 of the MS., around the border are these expressions :—

SLJT   SFILT   TRIKT   PPMRJT   ḤLFT   ILFT   ḤLIFT

§ 43. FOR A WOMAN IN TRAVAIL.

Write upon a leaf and give her to swallow:—' In the name of the Father and the Son, Lazarus, come forth '[1]; or this (expression), ' Mary bore Christ, and he silenced all natures.'

§ 44. FOR MILK NOT TO SPOIL.

In the name of the Father, the Son, and the Holy Ghost. By the name of Mar Artemus and Balnus, by these holy names, they who were in the cavern of the earth for forty years, and were praying to God on this account, that He might be the protector of this milk, that cream may be therein as the sand of the seas; by that angel which formeth the foetus in the womb of their mothers: so may there form and be healthy the milk of A. . . . B., and like Gihon [2] may its curds and cream [3] come, also as a fountain that flows in Eden [4], by the adored and glorious Name of the Living God. So be it. Amen !

Say the benediction [5] over the salt, and give (of it) to the cow to eat, and part of it (cast) into the fire, and part of it into the milk.

§ 45. BINDING THE NAVEL.

Say the benediction over the egg, and give him to eat.

In the name of the Father, the Son, and the Holy Ghost. I bind the navel of A., the son of B., like a bull in the yoke, like a horse by the bridle, and like a dead person in the grave, and like a bird in the snare and in the net. I bind his navel by that power with which Elijah the Prophet bound the heavens for three years and six months, so that no rain

---

[1] John xi. 43.   [2] Gen. ii. 13.

[3] ܪܒܝܐ fresh butter (not boiled), and so would not keep ; ܚܘܬܪܐ is butter boiled and put in jugs, able to keep for months.

[4] *Cf.* Gen. ii. 10.

[5] The proper place for this benediction is evidently immediately after the former heading, § 44.

came down upon the earth[1]. By that power shall come and be bound the navel of A., the son of B. By that power with which Mar Cyprian bound women who were with child, so that they should not bring forth, and barren women that they should not conceive, do I bind the navel of the one who carries this charm. So be it. Amen!

§ 46. THE ANATHEMA OF MAR SHALITA, WHICH IS OF AVAIL FOR THE EVIL SPIRIT.

In the name of the Father, the Son, and the Holy Ghost. The prayer, request, petition, and supplication of Mar Shalita, which he prayed and asked of God at the hour of martyrdom. He said: O my Lord, Jesus Christ, (as regards) every one who shall make mention of thy Holy Name, and of my name, thy servant Shalita, may no red spirit nor evil spirit approach him, (but may it be expelled) from[2] the body and from the soul of A., the son of B., by the prayer of blessed Mar Augin (Eugenius). Amen!

§ 47. BINDING THE MOUTH OF THE SPARROW AND THE MOUSE.

In the name of the Father, the Son, and the Holy Ghost. I bind the mouth of the eater, and of the mouse, and of the sparrow, and of the winged creature, and of the cattle. I bind them by the living Sign of the Cross of our Lord, and through the prayers of my Lady, the blessed Mary, and by Him who bound heaven, earth, the springs, and the rivulets, the cattle, the winged creature of heaven, and the worm. I bind the mouth of creeping things, of the eater, of the mouse, of the sparrow, and of the bird from off the crops of him who bears these writs. I bind them by Him who descended from heaven,

---

[1] Luke iv. 25; Jas. v. 17. *Cf.* 1 Kings xvii. 1, xviii. 1.

[2] If translated according to my foot-note in the text, it would be:—
' May no . . . . . evil spirit approach him, i. e. the body and soul of, &c.'

presenting the sacred mysteries [1]. I bind the mouth of the eater, of the mouse, of the sparrow, of the winged creature, and of the cattle; I bind them by the living Sign of the Cross of our Lord, through the prayer of my Lady, the blessed Mary, from the field of A., the son of B. Amen!

§ 48. BINDING THE FIRE FROM OFF THE STALKS AND STANDING CORN.

By the Divine Power which extinguished the fiery furnace from off those of the house of Hananiah, Azariah, and Mishael [2], may He extinguish the fire and the flame, that it burn not the heaps of corn and stalks, nor the house of A., the son of B.: by the Divine Power which extinguished the fiery furnace of Mar George, may He extinguish the fire and the flame, that it burn not, nor set light to the heaps of corn, or the stalks, nor to the house of the one who carries these writs. Furthermore, I bind, expel, and extinguish the iron, and again I bind the flint-stone [3], that fire may not proceed from them: I bind the fire that it shall not burn.

The winds and the whirlpools are the work of his Word: and Kedar shall be pastures [4]. He causes the winds to blow, and they cause the waters to descend [5]. I bind their hands and feet (i. e. of the incendiaries); their back shall always be bowed down. I bind the iron and the flint-stone, that no fire may proceed from them. By the Word which Elijah spake,

---

[1] The Holy Sacrament, Mass, &c.   [2] Dan. iii.

[3] Refers to the practice of rubbing steel against flint-stone, so as to produce sparks. The steel for this purpose is called in modern Syriac ܩܘܡܟܐ (Chakmak), not ܩܘܪܬܐ. The ܩܘܪܬܐ is a very hard yellow stone, sharp as a razor, often used to shave with; while ܩܘ (Kau) is the name for the cotton used in catching the spark. To make this ܩܘ, grass is burnt to cinders, and water is poured on the cinders; the water is allowed to stand for two days, after which it becomes quite yellow; cotton is soaked in it for a few hours; it is then dried, and becomes easily ignited.

[4] Cf. Isa. xxi. 16, xlii. 11, &c.   [5] Ps. cxlvii. 18.

who bound the heavens for three years and six months, so
that no rain came down upon the earth: by that selfsame
Word I bind the iron and the stone, that no fire shall come
out of them, that it may not kindle, nor burn the herbs or
the corn of A., the son of B.   Amen!

§ 49. For blood coming from the nostril.

Zechariah had his throat cut, and the fountain of waters[1]
was stopped.   So may the blood of A., the son of B., be
stopped.   Amen!

Write[2] with the blood of him (whose nose is bleeding) on
his forehead with a stalk of wheat.

§ 50. For boys not to cry.

In the name of the Father, the Son, and the Holy Ghost.
In the name of Jamlicha, and Maxinos, and Martlos, and
Serapion, and Johanis.

As those seven brothers who slept the sleep (of) 377 years[3],
so may A., the son of B., be at rest and sleep; yea, may he
sleep the sleep of the man of valour, by the prayer of the
prophets and apostles.   So be it.   Amen!

---

[1] *Cf.* Jer. ii. 13 ; Eccles. xii. 6 ; Zech. xiii. 1 ; Mark v. 29, &c.

[2] Probably, 'write' the preceding formula : 'Zechariah, &c.'

[3] Referring to seven noble youths of Ephesus who in the Decian
persecution concealed themselves in a cavern, in which they slept
for several centuries, then awoke for a short time only to expire.
Cf. the Koran (Sale's edit.), ch. xviii, entitled 'The Cave': 300, 309,
and 372 are the years of sleep according to the various versions, whilst
the number seven is doubtful as regards the sleepers.   Gibbon has the
story in one form, giving the name of one of the sleepers as Jamblichus.
Citing Gregory of Tours, *De Gloria Martyrum*, i. 9, the names of the seven
are given as Constantine, Dionysius, John, Maximian, Malchus, Mar-
tinian, and Serapion.   For the name Jamlicha or Jamblichus *cf.* 1 Chron.
iv. 34.   Other names are : Antoninus, Hexecostadianus, Martelius.

§ 51. FOR THE MAN UPON WHOM SORCERY HAD BEEN PRACTISED.

Jannes and Jambres [1] practised the magical arts; but they were unable to stand against Moses the prophet. So may there be annulled divination and the bonds of magic from off A., the son of B. So be it. Amen! Amen!

§ 52. THE ANATHEMA OF THE FATHERS [2], I. E. OF PARADISE, WHICH AVAILS FOR ALL PAINS.

In the name of the Father, the Son, and the Holy Ghost. By the prayer of the just and righteous Fathers, Paul, and Antonis (Antonius), and Makris (Macarius), and Arsanis (Arsenius), and Serapion, and Mar Paula of Shemishat, the blessed Enoch and Elijah, Mar John the Baptist, Mar John T'yaya, Mar John of Cashcar, Mar John Agubtaya, Mar John Kank'laya, Mar John Nach'laya, Mar John the Pastor, Mar John of Mobadra (Modra?) [3], Mar John the Golden [4], Mar John of Ṣusina (*sic*), Mar John bar Abgar, Mar John bar Martha, Mar John bar Edtha, Mar John Zoebi, Mar John of Dassan, Mar John the Evangelist, Mar John Chemulaya, Mar John of Azrak, Mar John of Jilu, Mar John of Urmiah, Mar John of Anzal, Mar John of Zana [5], Mar John

---

[1] 2 Tim. iii. 8. These two names (Gk. Ἰαννῆς and Ἰαμβρῆς) occur in the Hebrew garb of ינים (יונוס) and ימברים (ימרים or יומברום); *vide* Midrash Tanḥuma to Exodus xxxii. 1 on the words, 'And when the people saw that Moses delayed, &c.' They are supposed to be but another form of יוחני וממרא Joḥani (Johannes) and Mamre, the two chief magicians of Egypt at the time of Moses, to which a reference occurs in the Talmud, *T. Menahoth*, 85 a. This passage is interesting.

[2] For tne fuller list of Fathers, see the corresponding passage in Cod. B, § 5.

[3] City of Mesopotamia, not far from the river Tigris (Payne-Smith).

[4] Golden-mouthed, adding ܟܣܦܐ before ܦܘܡܗ: evidently Chrysostom, 'the golden-mouthed,' known as ܦܘܡܗ ܗܘ ܕܗܒ, ܣܝܡ ܦܘܡܗ.

[5] Jilu, Anzal, Zana are near Urmiah in Turkish Kurdistan. Urmiah ܐܘܪܡܝܐ or ܐܘܪܡܝ occurs as Urmia, Urumijeh, Urumijah, &c.

the question-answerer, Mar Azad, Mar Buchtazad, Mar Gushtazad, Mar Simeon of Shenna, Mar Abraham, Mar Georgis
the Martyr, and Mar Koriakas (Cyriacus) the Martyr, Mar
Augin (Eugenius) and all his order, and Mar Shalita and his
order, and Mar Dubina, chief of hermits, and the three
hundred of the exalted monastery of Beth Sidra, and Shamuni
with her sons, and the poor woman and the two sons of
Shushan, Mar Pityon, and Rabban Pityon, by the prayers
of Gaddi (Caddis), Makbi (Maccabeus), Tarsi (Thassi), Ḥebron
(Avaran), Ḥebṣon (Apphus)[1], Bacchus and Jonadab[2], Eleazar[3],
and Shamuni the martyr, Phebe[4], and Tabitha[5], and
Ansimus, daughter of kings, Martha[6], and Mary Magdalene[7],
and Mar Aḥa, and Mar 'Abd-īshō'. With these their names,
and of those others that exist, I bind, anathematize, expel,
and extirpate all abominable actions, revenge, and evil spirits,
and all the wiles of cursed devils devoted to destruction[8],
from the body and from the soul of A., the son of B. So be
it. Amen!

§ 53. CUTTING[9] OUT THE ITCH (OR 'BOIL')[10].

Say the benediction over ashes three times.

In the name of the Father, the Son, and the Holy Ghost.
O Itch, brazen serpent! Who is it that showed thee upon the

---

[1] These five are the names of the five sons of Mattathias (*see* 1 Macc.
ii. 1-5).

[2] Bacchus and Jonadab are given in Wright's *Cat. of Syriac MSS. in B.M.*
(p. 547), 'written in a later hand on the margin', as two of the seven
sons of Shamuni, the other five being given as Makbi, Tarsi, Ḥebron,
Ḥebṣon, Gaddi (Gedad)—the very names of the sons of Mattathias.

[3] 2 Macc. vi. 18-31.   [4] Rom. xvi. 1.

[5] Acts ix. 36.   [6] Luke x. 38 sqq. ; John xi. 1 sqq.

[7] Matt. xxvii. 56 ; Mark xv. 40.

[8] According to one reading; or 'I excommunicate', according to the
other.

[9] ܩܘܣܡܐ might mean either 'section' (of a book) or 'cutting out'.

[10] In modern Syriac ܐܝܪܐ signifies a 'boil' or 'button', 'sore' or
'itch', and is practically identical with 'leprosy'. There may be a

Mountain of Tarmaka¹ and upon the dry log² (trunk or root
of tree)? Even so dry up the itch of A. B. Therefore
may God root thee up, and destroy thee for ever from thy
dwelling, and thy root from the land (i. e. surface) of the
members of A. B. In the name of I Am That I Am,
Almighty God, Adonai, Lord of Hosts, I cut it out on earth;
God heals it in heaven. So be it. Amen!

The finish. By the right hand of thy dominion, O my
Lord, Our Father which art in heaven, bless, O Lord, the
bearer of these writs: protect, O Lord, the bearer of these
writs: support the bearer of these writs: shield, O Lord, the
bearer of these writs: help, O Lord, the bearer of these writs:
may thy mercies and the compassion of thy Godhead be
continually poured out in abundance upon the one who bears
these writs, now, and at all times, for ever and ever. Amen!

§ 54. DETAILS (METHOD OF RECKONING) CONCERNING SICK
PERSONS, FROM WHAT SOURCE THE SICKNESS COMES UPON THEM.

In the name of our Lord, I write the details (method of
reckoning) concerning sick persons, from what source (the
sickness) comes upon them.

Take the numerical value of his name, and the name of his
mother, and subtract³ (the number) 9 in each case⁴

legend that the 'serpents' of Num. xxi were in reality the plague of
'leprosy', which was sent as a punishment for slander, as in the case of
Miriam, the sister of Moses (Num. xii. 1,2, 10). In Deut. xxviii. 27 we have
botch, scab, and itch (ܒܝܪ) in juxtaposition, whereas 'leprosy' is
always rendered ܒܝܪ in the Syriac (Scriptures). According to Rabbi
Hoshya, of Sichnin, in the name of R. Levi, the serpent was cursed with
leprosy, seeing that it is spotted and speckled (Midrash Rabba to Genesis
iii. 15).

¹ *Cf.* p. 50, B 44 'Mark of Tarmaka'
² Evidently referring to Moses putting the brazen serpent upon the dry
pole: Num. xxi. 6-9; John iii. 14, 15.
³ ܐܪܦܢ might equally well mean 'divide', for the Syrians did not
divide as we do, but by the process of 'subtraction'
⁴ It has been suggested to me that this might mean: Divide by 9 so
many times till one 9 or less than 9 remains.

If 1 remains, (it implies that) on the first day of the week
(Sunday) the illness began ; at sunset the Evil Eye took a hold
on him from the head, and from the shoulder, and from the
neck.   Nine days it lasts.

[In] the monastery of Mar John [you will find] [1] the
prescription (lit. ' writing ') for the Evil Eye.

If 2 remains, (it implies that) on the second day of the
week (Monday), at the new-moon, the malady commences,
(arising) from his stomach, and from his back, and from his
heart, and from his entire body.   His illness is from God.
Three days it lasts.

[In] the monastery of Peter and Paul [you will find] the
prescription (lit. ' writing ') for every kind (of illness).

If 3 remains, (it implies that) on the third day of the week
(Tuesday) the warm and dry sickness (took hold of him) : the
pestilential atmosphere (lit. ' the air of devils ') fell upon him.
Let him bathe in water and butter : make three coils of his
clothes, put one under his head, one on his right, and one on
his left.   Sixteen days it lasts.

[In] the monastery of Mar 'Abd-īshō' [you will find] the
prescription (lit. ' writing ') : I will lift up mine eyes unto
the mountains [2].

And if you have 4 remaining (it implies that) on the fourth
day of the week (Wednesday) was the atmosphere of the
devils.   He crossed the water, and did not call upon the name
of the Living God : there is, further, the Evil Spirit (which
caused the sickness).   Let him give alms to the orphans.
Seventeen days it lasts.

[In] the monastery of Mar Shalita [you will find] the
prescription (lit. ' writing ') for the Evil Spirit.

---

1 This is the only meaning we can assign to this and the following
similar passages.

2 Cf. Ps. cxxi. 1.

If 5 remains to you, (it implies that) on the fifth day of the week (Thursday) the illness began from over-feeding, and for not having called upon the name of our Lord. The atmosphere of demons fell upon him, and he has, further, the spirit of devils. Sixteen days it will last.

[In] the monastery of Mar Sergius [you will find] the prescription (lit. 'writing') for one who has devils within him, (sprung) from the blood of black hens.

If you have 6 remaining, the sickness began on Friday from being close to a smell. The malady originated from his head, from his heart, and from his chest. He requires a charm of two lengths. Twelve days it will last.

[In] the monastery of my Lady Mary [you will find] the prescription for lunacy.

If 7 remain to you, (it implies that) on the Sabbath Day (Saturday) the creeping fear[1] fell upon him; the sickness (originating) from the lower part of his body[2], and from his heart, and from his head, the trembling came upon him. Fetch earth from seven ways, and from seven tombs[3], and from seven springs of water, and water (from) under the mill, and read over them (the portion) :—'In the beginning.'[4] Then let him bathe in them. Twenty-one days the illness will last.

[In] the monastery of Mar George [you will find] the prescription for fear and trembling.

If 8 remains to you, (it means that) on Wednesday he had an evil vision of having been smitten by the Satan. His entire system is deranged. Twenty days it will last.

[In] the monastery of Mar Ezekiel [you will find] the prescription for the evil spirit.

---

1 Or fear (called) ܠܝܘܐ ; *cf.* Deut. xxxii. 24, and Micah vii. 17.

2 Perhaps the Latin *cauda*.

3 ܩܒ̈ܪܐ ܒܝܬ 'sepulchres', not burying-grounds: *cf.* Matt. xxiii. 29.

4 Most likely St. John, ch. i.

If you have 9 remaining, (it means that) on Friday he was sitting on a clod of mud or on a drain; he did not pronounce (lit. 'cause to come, take') the name of God. Under the threshold of the house the atmosphere of Zarduch fell upon him. Nineteen days it will last.

[In] the monastery of Mar Cyriacus [you will find] the prescription as you wish (i.e. for whatever illness you like).

This manuscript is finished in the blessed month Tammuz, on the 30th day thereof, in the year 2114 of the blessed Greeks [1]. Amen!

This manuscript is finished under the roof (or 'bishopric') of Mar George. Amen!

This manuscript has been written in the name (by order) of the blessed young man, the beautiful branch, Tarveran, son of the deceased Zarunda (?) [2]; his mother is called Elizabeth (?) [3], of the blessed village Shibani. Any one into whose hands this manuscript shall fall, and he does not return it to its owner, shall be under the ban of the 318 Fathers. So be it. Amen!

This manuscript is finished at the hands of the feeble, sinning, wicked, impure, and infirm one, that is, the priest George, son of the deceased Zaia, of the blessed village Shibani. Amen, Amen!

---

[1] Corresponding to 1802-3.

[2] MS. faulty. Payne-Smith has ܪ݊ܘܿ, Zarvandades, nom. duorum e duodecim Magis qui Dūm nostrum adorabant.

[3] MS. faulty; probably Elizabeth.

CODEX B

§ 1. BY THE POWER OF OUR LORD, JESUS CHRIST, WE BEGIN TO WRITE (THE WORK ON) 'THE PROTECTION OF MANKIND'.

Foremost above all things, that prayer which our Lord taught his disciples[1]: Our Father which art in heaven, hallowed be thy name. Thy Kingdom come, and thy will be done, as in heaven, so on earth. Give us the bread which we need for the day. Forgive us our trespasses and sins as we also forgive those who sin against us. And lead us not into temptation, but deliver us from evil: for Thine is the Kingdom, the power, and the glory, for ever and ever. Amen.

§ 2. THE PRAYER OF OUR FATHER ADAM.

We acknowledge Thee, O Lord of All: and thee, O Jesus Christ, we glorify, for thou art the reviver of our bodies, and the redeemer of our souls.

§ 3. THE PRAYER OF THE HOLY ANGELS.

O holy God, holy Mighty One, holy Immortal: O our Lord, have pity upon us: O our Lord, receive thou our petition: O our Lord, be gracious unto thy servants who bear these writs (amulets). Amen!

§ 4. THE HOLY GOSPEL OF OUR LORD JESUS CHRIST, THE PREACHING OF JOHN [2].

In the beginning was the Word, and that Word was with God. And this Word was God, and the same was in the beginning with God. And everything was by his hand, and without him there was not one thing (made) of that which

---

[1] Matt. vi. 9-13 ; Luke xi. 2-4.   [2] John i. 1-5.

was. In him was life, and the life was the light of men.
And that light shineth in the darkness, and the darkness
preventeth it not.

By the power which is concealed in those Ten Holy Words
(Commandments) of the glorified Godhead, and by the name
I Am That I Am, Almighty God, Adonai, Lord of Hosts,
may there be expelled, extirpated, chased and dashed in
pieces all those accursed and rebellious demons, devils, and
phantoms, and all (evil) working : all temptations, unclean
spirits, cruel dreams and dark apparitions : fear and trembling,
terror and surprise, dread, anxiety, and weeping to excess :
the fever-horror and the three-days' one, aye, all kinds of
fever, and febrile ills, inflammations, burnings and piercings :
also (when) the child troubles its mother with the pains
of travail : and as for tumors and pestilences, the designs of
demons, the wiles of apparitions, and the accidents of devils,
sweet and harsh musical sounds, and the sweet and harsh
noises, all pains and all sicknesses, all wounds and all opposi-
tions, surprises, revenges and Zarduch, and all (evil) working, the
nine sicknesses, and Miduch, and the demon and Lilith, [may
they all be expelled] from the body and members of him that
beareth these writs.   Amen !

By that Divine power which healed the mother-in-law of
Simon Peter of the fever-horror [1], and cast the devil out
of the governor, and by that Will and glorious command
that commanded the fish and it spewed out Jonah, and drove
Adam out of Paradise : (by that voice) that cried out on the
Cross, by that Power that stopped the sun, and caused the
moon to stand still, and by those who cry out night and day,
' Holy, Holy, Holy is the Lord, God All-powerful, heaven
and earth are full of his glory.'   By the prayers, too, of
Hezekiah, and by the prayers of my Lady, the blessed Mary,
and of Mar John, the forerunner of Christ, may he who
bears on his person these writs be helped and healed. Amen !

---

1 Matt. viii. 14, 15 ; Mark i. 30, 31 ; Luke iv. 38, 39.

And as ye go, preach, saying, The Kingdom of Heaven is at hand. Heal the sick, cleanse the lepers, and cast out the devils: freely ye have received, freely give[1], and preach my gospel to all the world. He who will believe and be baptized will live, but he who does not believe shall be condemned. Signs shall follow those who believe these things.

By my name devils shall go forth, and they (the believers) shall speak with new tongues: they shall take serpents in their hands, and though they shall drink the deadly poison, it shall not hurt them; and they shall place their hands upon the sick, and they shall be cured.

He (Christ) said: There has been given unto me all dominion in heaven and on earth: and as my Father has sent me, thus do I send you. Go, then, teach all the peoples and baptize them in the name of the Father, Son, and Holy Ghost: and instruct them to observe all that I have commanded you. And lo, I am with you all the days, even unto the end of the world. Amen!

§ 5. THE ANATHEMA OF PARADISE[2], WHICH IS OF AVAIL
FOR ALL SICKNESSES AND DISEASES.

In the name of the Father, Son, and Holy Ghost. In like manner as the Lord, the All-powerful God, planted the Garden in Eden, and placed therein a large fountain, and distributed from it the four rivers, Gihon, Pishon, Daklat (Hiddekel), and the great river Euphrates[3]; and they sprang forth and watered the four corners of the world: and just as none of humankind can withstand and prevent them, so, O Lord, God of Might, let not evil men, cursed and deceitful demons, hinderers and devils, fear and trembling and dread, and all sicknesses and diseases have power over [but let them be driven away from][4] the body of him who carries these writs. Amen!

---

1 Matt. x. 7, 8.   2 *Cf.* Cod. A, § 52.
3 Gen. ii. 8-14.   4 *Vide* note on text.

By Him who looketh at the earth, and it trembles, and at the fountains of water and they turn to blood: by that Presence which dwelt upon Mount Sinai: by the praises of the Cherubim, by the sanctification of the Seraphim, by the powers and sovereignties, by the principality and dominion [1], by the nine regiments of angels who glorify that Chariot upon which shineth the glorious majesty of the Living God. By the creation of Adam and Eve, by the offering of Abel and Jephthah, by the beauty of Seth [2], by the revelation of Enosh [3], by the translation of Enoch [4], by the offerings of the just and righteous patriarchs, by the ark of Noah, by the priests of Melchizedek, by the faith of Abraham, by the sacrifice of Isaac, by the ladder which Jacob saw, by the staff of Moses, by the priesthood of Aaron, by the chastity [5] of Joshua, son of Nun, by the zeal of Phineas, by the strength of Judah, by the prayer of Hannah, by the Nazaritism of Samuel, by the mantle of Elijah, by the garment of Elisha [6], by the Vision which Isaiah saw in the Temple, by the Chariot which Ezekiel saw, by the den of Daniel, by the furnace of the children, by the mysteries which Jonah, the son of Mattai, typified in the belly of the fish [7], by the annunciation (revelation) of John, by the silence of Zechariah, by the coming of our Redeemer, by the Power which descended and dwelt in the Virgin, by his birth in the flesh, by his holy baptism, by his pure fasting, by the Hosannas which the children cried out to him (on his way to Jerusalem), by his great passion on the Cross which was on Golgotha, by the nails and the spears which were fixed in him, by the tomb in which

---

1 *Cf.* Eph. vi. 12.

2 In the Liturgy, &c. Seth is spoken of as 'beautiful'.

3 Gen. iv. 26.   4 Gen. v. 22–24; Heb. xi. 5.

5 Celibacy; *lit.* 'virginity', used both of males and females; *cf.* Rev. xiv. 14.

6 *Cf.* Cod. A, § 38.

7 Jonah regarded as a type of Christ; three days in the belly of the fish to typify the three days of Christ in the tomb.

he was placed, by his resurrection after three days, by his
ascension to Heaven, by his seat on the right hand (sc. of
God), by the Holy Ghost which he sent to his holy apostles,
by the preaching of the apostles, by the massacre of martyrs,
by the blood of the confessors, by the gospel of those who
planted (the tidings), by the tears of hermits, by the goodly
service of the monks and those who dwell in holes, by the
prayer and petition of all who have been pleasing and are
pleasing to thee, O Lord, God of Might, we bind, and
anathematize, and expel, and prevent, and distance evil demons
and accursed devils, rebellious Satans, wicked and envious
people, the wiles of Emirs, fear, trembling, fright and
surprise, anxiety and heaviness, the evil and envious eye,
sweet and harsh sounds, evil spirits, all calamities and all
opposition, [we expel these] from the body and members
of the man who bears these writs. Amen!

By the prayers of my Lady, the blessed Mary, mother of
Christ, our Redeemer and Saviour, and of the ambassador
Mar John the Baptist, by the sufferings of Peter and
Paul, and the four Evangelists, Matthew, Mark, Luke, and
John, and by the right-hand of Mar Thomas, the Apostle,
who touched the side of our Redeemer, and Mar Stephen,
the first of martyrs, by Mar Deodorus and Mar Theodorus,
and Mar Nestoris (Nestorius) and (by the prayers) of the
Syrian teachers, Mar Aprem, Mar Narsai, Mar Abraham,
Mar Job, Mar Sharbel, and all their companions. Amen!

And by the prayers of our spiritual fathers, Abba Paulus,
and Abba Antonis, and Abba Makris (Macarius), and Abba
Arsanis (Arsenius), and Abba Evagris, and Abba Paladis, and
Abba Ur, and Abba Pasis, and Abba Isaiah, and Abba Paula,
the Simple, and Abba Moses of Cush, and Abba Piyur,
Superior, and Abba Serapion, and Abba Marcus of Tarmaka,
and Abba Aginus, and Abba Chronicus, and Abba Sarmita,
and (by the prayers) of all their companions. Amen!

And by the prayers of those of the Eastern and Western

i

(peoples) :—Mar Augin, and Mar Shálita, and Mar Sargis
(Sergius), and Mar Bacchus, and Mar Shahak, and Mar
Cunyapa, and Mar Uchama, and Mar 'Abda, and Titus, and
Mar Joseph of Yudablad, and Mar Denḥa, and Mar Babi of
Semka, and Mar Sargis of Wăda, and Mar Cudau of Beth
Hālē, and Mar Jonah of Inbar, and Mar Simeon of Estūma,
and Mar Gabriel of Serapa, and Mar Gavruna, and Mar
Jacob who was cut in pieces, and Mar Shabur, and Mar
Kurta, and the martyrs of the monastery of Edrē, and
Shamuni and her sons, and the poor woman and her two
children, and Bar Sahadē, and Mar Maruta and his uncle,
and Abdulla of Dūchrana, and Mar Gushtazad, and Mar
Simeon of Shenna, and Mar Isaac, and Mar Georgis, and the
martyrs of the mount of Niḥ, and Mar Barchisu, and Mar
Barkusri, and Mar Elia, and Mar Gabriel, and Mar Michael,
and Rabban Hurmizd, and Mar Jacob of Beth Abhē, and
Rabban Pityōn of Dassan, and Rabban Joseph the seer, and
Mar Kardagh, and Mar Tālya, and Mar 'Abd-īshō' the monk,
and Mar Shalita of Rashina, and Mar Joseph, and Rabban
Aaron, and Mar Pappa, and Mar Sāba the physician, and
Mar Zĕura, and Mar Koma[1], and Mar Domestyanē, and Mar
Domat, and Mar Aḥa, and Mar Gniva, and Mar Abraham of
Cashcar, and Mar Koriakos (Cyriacus), the boy and his
mother, my Lady Julietta, and Mar Zaia, and Mar Azīza, and
Mar Shūḥa-l'ishō'[2], and Mar Tamsis, and Mar Cochva, and
Mar Gaussa: by the prayers of Mar John the Baptist,
and Mar John the Evangelist, and Mar John of Ilumaya,
and Mar John the Seer, and Mar John the Pastor, and Mar
John of Apma, and Mar John of Liyaya, and Mar John of
Shemishat, and Mar (John)[3] of Susana, and Mar John bar
Malcha, and Mar John bar Zoebi, and Mar John bar Evagra,

[1] Or ' Boma '; the first letter in MS. is indistinct.
[2] Wright spells : Shūbha le-Yĕshua. *Cf.* the name   Praise-God Barebone.
[3] Supply ' John ' after ' Mar '.

and Mar John bar Narsai, and Mar John of Hirta, and Mar
John Saba, and Mar John of Ashnaz, and Mar John of Blūk,
and Mar John of Anzal, and Mar John of Hetrē, and Mar
Elia Abuḥalim, and Mar Shamli the Just, with all the just
and righteous ones, and the companies of these names of
saints, they themselves and their disciples, those who have
died and those who are still living, as for the names of all
of them, you know them as they are inscribed in the books.
By this ban shall be bound, anathematized, expelled, prevented
and despatched all cursed and rebellious demons, Satans and
devils.

§ 6. The anathema of my Lady, the blessed Mary,
which is of avail for sick persons.

The prayer, request, petition, and supplication of her full
of grace, my Lady, the blessed Mary, mother of Christ, our
Redeemer and Preserver: at the time when she came down
from the Mount of Eden, and from near Paradise, and came
to the city Jerusalem, and when our Lord, having entered,
there arose the noise of babes and children who cried out
and shouted, saying [1] : 'Hosanna in the highest : Hosanna to
the son of David : blessed be he that cometh in the name of
the Lord!' and all the multitudes (lit. assemblies) were
carrying branches of trees, and were singing unto our Lord
while he was riding on the colt which was tamed, and it was
praised by the multitudes, who placed their garments before
our Lord : and (when) he saw Mary, his mother, and said
unto her, O mother, whence comest thou? and she replied
and said : From the country of Eden I come, in order to ask
of thee one request. Our Lord answered and said unto her,
I will grant thee thy request, and more than thy request.
Thereupon my Lady Mary asked on behalf of the sick, that
they may be healed, and regarding the sorely pressed, that
they may be enlarged, yea exceedingly. [Thus did she speak]

_____
[1] Cf. Matt. xxi and Mark ix.

O my Lord, my Son, and my Salvation!   [I pray] for the
barren among women that they may bear : that, by thy power,
O Lord, they who bear may bring forth sons who will be
a blessing, and daughters of righteousness : that the barren
may conceive, the sick be healed, and those who are sore
pressed receive enlargement; and that the women who bear,
those whose children are strangled by this deceitful demon,
who for a man assumes the form of women, and for women
the form of men, [I pray, that they may be protected against
her] who assumes the form of a hateful woman, whose appearance enslaves, and strikes the fruit of the womb, and takes
captive weak minds after its wickedness, as though she would
be unto them a help.   People call her by many names : some,
by that of ' the strangling mother of boys ' : some, Miduch :
some Zarduch.   And now, O my Lord, listen to the prayer of
the one who bore thee, and prevent and expel this demon that
she do not injure nor approach thy servants who carry this
invocation.   [I pray] by thy great and terrible Name, and by
the power of thy Invisible Father who is concealed in thee,
and by the power of the Holy Ghost which dwelleth within
thee, and by the power of the Cherubim and the Seraphim
and the Heavenly Hosts, those who bear and glorify the
Throne of thy Divinity : and by the prayers of the prophets,
apostles, martyrs, confessors, fathers, and teachers.   So be it.
Amen !

§ 7. The anathema of Mar 'Abd-īshō', the monk and hermit.

The prayer, request, petition, and supplication of Mar
'Abd-īshō', the monk and hermit of God, who was among the
dumb beasts on the Friday, which is the Passion (sc. day) of
our Lord and Redeemer, at the time when the evil spirit, in
the likeness of a hateful woman of dark appearance, was
coming down from the Mount of Eden, and she appeared
unto him, and called him by name, 'Abd-īshō' : and he said

unto her, Who art thou? She replied and said:—I am
a woman, and will be your partner. Thereupon the saintly
Mar 'Abd-īshō', as soon as he perceived that she was a wicked
and unclean spirit, bound her, and cursed and tied her up,
saying: You are not empowered to show your might and
strength and craft over the men-servants and women-servants
of God who carry these formulae. And furthermore, I conjure
thee by Him at whom angels and men tremble, that if thou
hast any other names, reveal it to me, and show me, and hide
it not. She said unto him: ' I will reveal it unto thee, though
I desire it not. I have twelve other names. Whosoever will
write them and hang them upon himself, or place them in
his house, his house will I not enter, nor [approach] his
children. First, Miduch: second, Edilta: third, Mouelta:
the fourth they call Lilita and Malvita and the Strangling
Mother of boys.' Thereupon the saintly Mar 'Abd-īshō', as
soon as he perceived that she was an evil and unclean spirit,
bound her, and cursed her, and tied her up, and said unto her,
You are not empowered to show your might and strength and
craft over the servant of the Living God who carries these
writs: and furthermore, I conjure you by the One, at whom
angels and men tremble, that if you have any other names,
reveal it to me, and show me, and hide nothing from me.
She replied unto him: I will reveal it unto thee, though
I desire it not. I have twelve other names. Whosoever will
write them and hang them upon himself, his house will I not
enter, nor do harm unto his wife, nor unto his children, nor
unto anything which he hath or will have. My first name
(is) Gĕos: second, Edilta: third, Lāmbros: fourth, Martlos:
fifth, Yāmnos: sixth, Sāmyos: seventh, Domos: eighth,
Dirba: ninth, Apiton: tenth, Pegogha: eleventh, Zarduch,
Lilita, Malvita, and the Strangling Mother of boys. Then
the saintly Mar 'Abd-īshō' said unto her: I bind you off him
who carries these writs in the name of the God of Gods and
Lord of Lords, and in the name of the Being who is from ever-

lasting : may there be bound, doomed, and expelled all accursed
and rebellious demons, and all evil and envious persons, and
all calamities from off him who carries these writs !

§ 8. The anathema of Mar George, the glorious
martyr, which is of avail against fear.

The prayer, request, petition, and supplication of Mar
George, the glorious martyr, which he prayed, requested, and
petitioned before God at the time of his martyrdom. He
put his knees in (the attitude of) prayer, and said : O Lord,
God of Hosts, I request and petition thy grace, grant me this
demand, that every one who shall make mention of thy Holy
Name, Lord Jesus, and my name, thy servant George, no
harm shall happen unto him carrying these writs, nor fear,
nor trembling, nor surprise, nor evil visions, nor the evil and
envious eye. Remove from him pains and sicknesses, fear
and trembling, and those visions which come by night and
by day : and every one who writes and hangs upon himself
thy Holy Name—Lord Jesus Christ, and my name, thy
servant George, may there be unto him neither fear nor
trembling, nor anxiety, nor surprise, nor visions of hard
dreams, nor dark phantasies, nor the evil and envious eye :
but let there be bound, doomed, and expelled all pains and
sicknesses, and calamities from off him who carries these
writs, and grant him his goodly requests from out of the
Treasure-house of thy Compassion, by the prayers of those on
high (angelic beings) and the supplication of those below, and
by the anathema of Mar George, the glorious martyr, and
Mar Simon Peter, and Mar Babi, and Mar Cyprian, and Mar
Sassan, and of all the martyrs and saints of our Lord, for
ever and ever. Amen !

§ 9. Concerning the Evil and Envious Eye.

The Evil Eye went forth from the eye of the heart, and
the angel Gabriel met her, and said unto her, ‘Whither goest

エラー

thou, O daughter of destruction?' She replied unto him:
'I am going to destroy men and women, male and female
children, and the souls of beasts and fowls.' The angel
Gabriel addressed her: 'Have you not been to Paradise and
seen the great God—Him whom thousands upon thousands,
and myriads upon myriads of angels surround? By his
Name may there be bound by me, and I bind you, O Evil
and Envious Eye, the eye of strangers, the eye of those
dwelling in our midst, the eye of people far off, the eye of
those who are near, the green-coloured eye, and the blue-
coloured eye, the dark-grey eye, and the tearful eye, and the
eye of the seven evil ones, from off the body and members,
from off the servants, from off the sheep and oxen, from off
the vineyards and fields of him who carries these writs,
through the prayers of my blessed Lady Mary, and of
Mar John the Baptist. So be it. Amen!'

§ 10. [BAN FOR] THE FOLD OF CATTLE.

'Seven accursed brothers, accursed sons! destructive ones,
sons of men of destruction! Why do you creep along on
your knees and move upon your hands?' and they replied:
'We go on our hands, so that we may eat flesh, and we
crawl along upon our hands, so that we may drink blood.'
As soon as I saw it, I prevented them from devouring, and
I cursed and bound them in the name of the Father, Son,
and Holy Ghost, saying: 'May you not proceed on your way,
nor finish your journey, and may God break your teeth and
cut the veins of your neck and the sinews thereof, that you
approach not the sheep nor the oxen of the person who
carries [sc. these writs]! I bind you in the name of Gabriel
and Michael. I bind you by that angel who judged the
woman that combed (the hair of) her head on the eve of
holy Sunday. May they vanish as smoke from before the
wind for ever and ever. Amen!'

§ 11. Concerning lunacy.

In the name of the Father, Son, and Holy Ghost.
O Lord, God of Hosts, and Possessor of all! Thou hast
said in thy Gospel, that 'every one who asketh receiveth,
and he that seeketh findeth, and it shall be given unto him [1]'
So also now, O Lord, God of Hosts, I ask of thee on behalf
of thy servant who carries these writs (regarding) the bitter
sickness which is called 'lunacy': mayest thou send the
angel which bears words of compassion and of healing, and
may he who carries these formulae be healed from the sickness
of lunacy, through the prayer of Mar Jacob [2], who was killed
by the violent Jews with a fuller's club at the time when he
suffered martyrdom. Thou, O Lord, aid him carrying these
writs. Amen!

§ 12. [Of avail] before kings, rulers, prefects, satraps, and chiefs.

In the name of the Father, Son, and Holy Ghost.
I clothed myself in secret with the Father, and openly
I am wrapped with the Son, and mysteriously doth the
Holy Spirit dwell within me: verily I fear no evil. [Mary]
met Elizabeth, and the boy leapt in her womb [3] over against
the boy of Mary, through the mystery which was between
them. As regards the one who beholds the bearer of these
writs, I bind, and doom, and chase, and annihilate him by
the word which our Lord said unto his disciples: 'Whatsoever ye shall bind on earth shall be bound in heaven [4].'
Thus, O Lord, God of Hosts, I bind, curse, chase, annihilate
kings, rulers, prefects, governors, centurions, magistrates,
sub-officers, and officers, men and women, that they shall not
speak evilly and hatefully with the one who carries these
writs; by that power and by that garment with which

[1] Matt. vii. 7, 8 ; Luke xi. 9, 10.   [2] James, called the brother of Jesus.
[3] Luke i. 41.   [4] Matt. xviii. 18 and xvi. 19.

Alexander, the son of Philip, was clothed : he who subdued the whole earth : thus, O Lord, God of Hosts, may he who carries these writs be clothed in the garments of victory and salvation before kings, lords, rulers, prefects, and magistrates. So be it. Amen !

This book is finished by the hand of the feeble one [1], Daniel, son of the priest Cushābā of Alkoosh, and unto God be the glory.

CODEX C

§ 1. BY THE POWER OF OUR LORD WE WRITE THE BOOK OF PROTECTION, AMEN ! IN THE NAME OF THE FATHER, THE SON, AND THE HOLY GHOST, THE HOLY GOSPEL OF OUR LORD, JESUS CHRIST, THE PREACHING OF JOHN [2] :—

[*Cf.* A, §§ 4, 13, 33, and B, § 4.]

In the beginning was the Word, and that Word was in the beginning with God, and God was [the Word]. In the beginning it was with God. And all was by his hand, and without him there was not one thing that existed. In him was life; and the life was the light of men. That light lighteth the darkness, which overcame it not.

By the power of those Ten Holy Words of the Lord God, by the name, I am that I am, God Almighty, Adonai, Lord of Hosts, I bind, excommunicate and destroy, I ward off, cause to vanish, all evil, accursed, and maddening (lit. 'misleading') pains and sicknesses, adversaries, demons, rebellious devils, also the spirits of lunacy, the spirit of the stomach, the spirits of the heart, the spirits of the head, the spirits of the eyes, the ills of the stomach, the spirit of the teeth, also the evil and envious eye, the eye that smiteth and pitieth

---

[1] This last page is torn : *vide* note in text.   [2] i. 1–5.

not, the green coloured eye, the eye of every kind, the eye of all spirits of pain in the head[1], pain on one side of the head, sweet and soft (doleful) pulsations, seventy-two such sweet and mournful noises, also the fever, cold and hot, visions fearful and false dreams, as are by night and by day; also Lilith, Malvita, and Zarduch, the dissembling (or 'compelling') demon, and all evil pains, sicknesses, and devils, bound by spell, from off the body and soul, the house, the sons and daughters of him who beareth these writs, Amen, Amen!

§ 2. The Ban of Mar George, the Martyr.
[Cf. A, § 5, B, § 8.]

In the name of the Father, the Son, and the Holy Ghost. The prayer, petition, and supplication of Mar George, the triumphant martyr, which he prayed and asked of God, the Saviour, at the time of martyrdom, placing his knee in (the attitude of) prayer, and said: O Lord God, All-powerful, as for every one who will make mention of thy Holy Name, O Lord, Jesus Christ, and the name of Georgis, may there not come to him either terror, trembling, anxiety, or anger, nor one of the evil pains, sicknesses, accursed demons that lead astray; rebellious Satan and envious evil ones; fearful visions and the faces of evil devils, demons, and the evil spirit; the eye of all wicked men and rebellious ones; nor fear, trembling, visions demoniacal, fright, bonds of magic; nor Lilith and Zaduch, the demon Malvita, mother of strangled children, boys and girls, the souls of the birds of heaven, all pains, evil sicknesses, rebellious ones, and visions fearful; nor the sweet sounds of the head, seventy-two evil sounds, and accursed adversaries that lead one astray, rebellious and envious, evil ones; may all wounds, and all dire sick nesses be kept away from the house of him who carries these scraps, Amen!

[1] For the spirit *Slahta*, *cf.* Talmud, *T. Sabbath*, 90 a ; *Gittin*, 68 b, &c.

§ 3. BINDING THE TONGUE OF THE RULER.
[Cf. A, §§ 6, 7 ; B, § 12.]

In the name of the Father, the Son, and the Holy Ghost.
By the name Gabriel, Michael, Ariel[1]; by the name
Michael, Azriel[2], Shamshiel, Harshiel, Sarphiel, Nuriel ; by
the name, I am that I am, God Almighty, Adonai, Lord of
Hosts; by the name Shamshiel, Susniel, Shamiel, Hiniel,
Zadikiel, Prukiel, Sahariel, Zakiel, Diniel, Eshiniel, Takifiel,
Gabriel, the mighty one, Shamshiel, Sahariel, Makiel,
Yomiel, Cukbiel, Shufiel, Mariel, Mehalalel, Zatriel, Umiel,
Hshahshiel, Tariel, Aziziel[3], Maniel, Samiel. By these holy
names, I bind, ban, stop the mouth and tongues of evil men,
jealous and wicked judges, emirs, satraps[4], governors, men
in authority, rulers and chiefs[5], executioners, prefects, the
foreigner, the gentile, the infidel. I bind the mouths of all
wicked judges, and all the sons of Adam and Eve, evil ones,
men, women, and children; I bind their tongues and lips,
their minds and thoughts, those of wicked ones, rebels, judges,
court-officials, and prefects; and the lips of the emir, prefects,
executioners, satraps, and rulers. I bind the tongues and
mouths of these wicked ones by that Word which our Lord
spake to his disciples : 'Whatever you shall bind on earth,
shall be bound in heaven.' I bind them from off him who
carries this charm !

[1] Cf. Ezra viii. 16.
[2] Cf. 1 Chron. v. 24.
[3] Cf. 1 Chron. xv. 20 ; Ezra x. 27.
[4] ܪ̈ܝܫܐ the same as ܪ̈ܝܫܐ 'satrap' ; cf. B, § 12 (heading).
[5] ܪ̈ܝܫܐ, ܪ̈ܝܫܐ, and ܪ̈ܝܫܐ seem to be different forms of one
and the same word; even ܪ̈ܝܫܐ occurs (Castelli), all connected with
root reg. (rex). In B, § 12 (heading), we have ܢ vice ܠ ; the probability
is, that ܢ or ܠ would be elided in pronunciation, and hence the form
ܪ̈ܝܫܐ ; whilst the careless speaker would add ܢ after ܣ and pronounce
ܪ̈ܝܫܐ.

§ 4. BINDING THE TEETH.
[*Cf.* A, § 17, B.M. § 66.]

Pronounce the blessing upon bread, Amen! In the name of the Father, the Son, and the Holy Ghost. In the name of the Living God, the Saviour, and Mar Thomas, Mar Pachumos[1], Mar Dormesan, Mar Horkus[2], Mar Harkles; by these holy names, we beseech thee, when the teeth chatter, or the evil spirit of the sweet sound (knocks), bless the bread; let him eat, and the teeth of A., the son of B., shall be healed. Amen, Amen!

§ 5. BINDING THE OX ASLEEP IN THE YOKE[3].
[*Cf.* A, § 24.]

In the name of the Father, the Son, and the Holy Ghost. By the prayer of Abba Jonah, Mar Shalita, Mar Milis, and Malchizedek[4], the priest and minister; and by the gentleness of all those at rest and laid low; by that Power which subjected heaven and earth, angels and men; so may this ox, that of A., the son of B., be subjected to its yoke; may the tread[5] be obedient to its yoke, to its master, by the prayer of my Lady, the blessed Mary, Mar John, Amen!

§ 6. THE ANT THAT FALLS UPON THE WHEAT.
[*Cf.* B.M. § 59.]

In the name of the Father, the Son, and the Holy Ghost. Go forth, O ant, from within this wheat, that of A., the son

[1] The fuller form for 'Pachum' (*cf.* A, § 5, where the name has ܘ not ܒ).

[2] From the script it is difficult to determine positively whether the name is 'Horrus' or 'Horkus'.

[3] If we read ܟ݉ܝܕ݉ܐ ܕܥ݉ܘܪ, the heading would run: 'Binding the ox that injures the cattle.'

[4] Gen. xiv. 18; Ps. cx. 4; Heb. v. 6.

[5] According to the text; if according to my note, 'may the ox be obedient, &c.'

of B., just as the children of Israel went forth into the wilderness, by the hand of Moses, the prophet; just as Adam went forth from the Garden, Jonah[1], Daniel from the dungeon, Hananiah from the fiery furnace, Noah from the ark; so, O ant, go forth from within the wheat of A., the son of B., by the Loving God, the Saviour, Amen, Amen!

§ 7. VERMIN [2] THAT COME UPON MEN.

Pronounce the blessing over the dust of the mole; cast it upon the vermin: (for) vermin that come upon possessions, bless the dust in the name of our Lord, Jesus Christ, and of Gabriel, chief of the holy Angels . . . [3]. He sowed sand and reaped sand, and did not tread down the standing-corn. In like manner, there shall not come any vermin upon A., the son of B., or the goats, or the oxen, in the name of the living Christ, Amen! So be it!

§ 8. BINDING THE FIRE FROM THE STONE JAR.
[*Cf.* A, § 48.]

Pronounce the blessing over wood. In the name of the Father, the Son, and the Holy Ghost. I bind this fire, this jar; this fire, and this wheat-flour; that it burn not, nor inflame[4], neither to the right nor to the left; may it be turned to its former and original nature; may it be bound by me through the four holy angels that bear the throne of the Living God, the Saviour! I bind this jar, that it kindle not to the right, nor burn to the left. May it be bound until I loosen it in the name of the Father, the Son, and the Living Spirit, Amen, Amen!

---

[1] The words 'from the belly of the fish', which we should expect, are omitted (*cf.* B, § 5).

[2] *Lit.* 'worms'.   [3] *See* note to Text.

[4] The original ܐܠܠ ܐܠܐ ܐܡܠ ܐܠܙ can scarcely stand; we should have to read something like ܐܠܡܠ ܐܠܐ ܐܡܠ ܐܠܙ, and I have translated accordingly.

LOOSENING THE FIRE OF THE JAR. Before you begin its
formula, recite three times the three words: 'Compassionate
me, God!' Recite three times: 'I am loosened · · · as the
fire that burneth.'

§ 9. IN THE NAME OF THE FATHER AND THE SON.
BINDING [1] THE BOIL (OR 'SCAB'). [*Cf.* A, § 53.]

In the name of the Father, the Son, and the Holy Ghost.
And Moses said unto his brethren, Go unto the land of
Egypt and make unto you a brazen serpent [2], and put it in
Midian; and one shall say, Let the children of Israel come,
and there shall dissolve (drop) this boil, this scab, by the
great Name of the Living God, by the name of the Glorified
Trinity, by the name of the nine regiments of the holy
angels. The Physician that heals all pains, the Healer of
all sicknesses and of all wounds, our Lord and God heals the
scab from the body of A., the son of B., Amen!

§ 10. BEFORE THE EMIR AND THE JUDGE.
[*Cf.* A, §§ 6, 7; B, § 12.]

In the name of the Father, the Son, and the Holy Ghost.
I bind and stop the mouths, the tongues, and lips, of wicked
and tyrannical people from off him who carries this order,
these writings; I bind them, excommunicate them, as the
horse (is bound) by the bridle, as the ox in the yoke, as
the dead in the grave, as the stars in the heavens, as the
fish in the sea; may they be bound by me by the ban [3]
falling from heaven upon the mouths and the tongues of

---

[1] If ܐܪܣܘܐ be the corrected reading, it is a form derived from רם
'bind'.

[2] *Cf.* Num. xxi. 8–9.

[3] The word ܒܠܘܬܐ in the text makes no sense whatsoever; I have,
therefore, proposed ܒܢܝܕܡܐ.

evil and violent men, emirs, kings, magistrates, rulers, tyrants, satraps, prefects, avaricious ones; in the name of Gabriel, Michael, in the name of Sarphiel, by the name, I am that I am, God Almighty, Adonai, Lord of Hosts, I bind the mouths and tongues of evil men, tyrants, military officials, and magistrates, all wicked and violent men, from him who bears this charm, by the Living Sign of the Cross of the Lord God, by the Name of the true Father [1], Amen!

§ 11. Binding the Prefects: Binding the Tongue.

[Cf. B.M. § 55.]

In the name of the Father, the Son, and the Holy Ghost.
ARGI, DRGI, BRGI, ZRGI, MRGI, HRGI [2].

*   *   *   *   *

And the Sun and Moon [3] may be with him who bears this charm, as God loved Moses, chief of the Hebrews, as God loved David, as God loved the prophet Daniel.

---

[1] For this expression, *see* John xviii. 38 and Acts x. 34.

[2] A comparison between this passage and the parallel passage in B.M, § 55 will reveal, in a manner perhaps more striking than in any other passage of this volume, how apparent errors in writing can baffle the most ingenious attempts at explanation. The scribe undoubtedly wrote down from memory or copied by rote, without in many cases even understanding the meaning of the words he put down; hence the jumble of unintelligible expressions.

Whether here ܐ݇ܦܪܘܕܝܛܐ (as one word) is 'Aphrodite' (Venus), and ܩܪܝܘ (the ܩܪܘܢܘ of B.M.) is 'Kronos' (Saturn), and they are two of the seven names derived from the stars, taken as representing guardian spirits, I will not determine. Even the word ܒܪ in B.M. may be ܕܗ݇ of C. Again, ܩܢܝܠܐ, ܒܪܐ may be the 'Artemus' of A, § 44, and ܣܝܡܘܢ may be Simon Magus. In this section we have, indeed, the Mystery of Magic.

[3] Though the MS. has ܢܘܗܪܐ 'Light', there is no doubt ܣܗܪܐ 'Moon' is the right word.

§ 12. Hurt [1] (?) to the back. [Cf. A, § 10·]

In the name of the Father, the Son, and the Holy Ghost; in the name of the Living God, the powerful One; the Saviour, compassionate and merciful, art thou; in thine abundant mercy, in thy lovingkindness, who in thy compassion didst silence, bidding the sea be still, and thou wast magnified; O Lord, by thy great Power, O mighty One, and Master (?) of all, assuage, I pray thee, this bitter stroke both from the back and side of A., the son of B., by the prayer of my Lady Mary, the blessed, Amen, Amen! So be it!

§ 13. Binding the navel [2]. [Cf. A, § 45.]

In the name of the Father, the Son, and the Holy Ghost. I bind the navel of A., the son of B., in the spot where it will never be moved, in its place, just as the ox in the yoke, the dead in the grave, the fish in the sea, the horse by the bridle, the camel by the cord, the star in the expanse of heaven, the tree which is fixed in the ground, so do I bind the navel of A., the son of B., by the living Sign of the Cross, Amen!

§ 14. Binding the wolf from off the cattle.
[Cf. A, § 35.]

In the name of the Father, the Son, and the Holy Ghost. The prayer and petition of Mar Daniel, the great prophet, at the time when they threw him into the den of lions, and he prayed, placing his knee in (the attitude of) prayer, and saying: O Lord God, the Powerful, we pray of Thee that as regards every one who shall make mention of Thy holy Name, O our Lord, Jesus Christ, and of my name Daniel,

---

[1] Wright renders the word 'lumbago'.

[2] If the word be ܪܕܗܝܙ (not ܪܕܗܝܙ), then read 'joint' here and in the other lines where 'navel' is mentioned. The same applies to the parallel passage in A, § 45.

neither the wolf, nor the bear, nor the panther, nor the sow, shall come to the lambs of him who carries these writs: the mouths, tongues, and teeth of the wolf, the bear, and the panther shall be closed against the goats, the sheep, the ox of him who bears this charm, Amen!

§ 15. BINDING THE DOG.   [*Cf.* A, § 21.]

In the name of the Father, the Son, and the Holy Ghost.

Mary and our Lord were walking on the way, and Mary was speaking unto our Lord, when lo a dog came up, and our Lord said unto Mary: See, I bind and stop them with chains of iron and stones of brass, and the iron shall come into their soul and into the flesh of the feet of these dogs of robbers, and they shall not bark at, nor have power over him who bears this charm, nor rob.

§ 16. ILLNESS [1] (?) OF THE STOMACH.   [*Cf.* A, § 25.]

In the name of the Father, the Son, and the Holy Ghost.

In the name of Pūka, Mar Pūka, Mar Nūka, Mar Pūka, O illness(?) of the stomach, Go forth from the stomach of A., the son of B., Go forth from . . . to the nerves, from (these) to the hands, the bones, from the bones to the nerves, from (these) to the hand, from (these) to the flesh, from (thence) to the skin, from the skin to the waste and dry rock, in the name of the Father, the Son, and the Holy Ghost, in the name of Mar Mamas, Mar Avin, by the living Sign of the great Cross, by the prayer of the blessed Mary, Amen!

§ 17. BINDING THE FEVER.   [*Cf.* A, § 28.]

In the name of the Father, the Son, and the Holy Ghost.

THSIMA [2] upon the fever of A., the son of B.; ASIMA upon the fever of A., the son of B.; ZUSIMA upon the fever

[1] If so, it is formed from 'malus'.
[2] I must leave these four names without any explanation; they are probably but mystical combinations of letters.

1

of A., the son of B.; ABRHIMA upon the fever of A. (the son of B.), by the prayer of blessed Mary, Mar Simon Peter, John, Paul the blessed Apostle, Matthew, Mark, Luke, and John, Amen!

§ 18. LOOSENING[1] THE FRUIT-CROPS FROM THE CATTLE.

In the name of the Father, the Son, and the Holy Ghost. KIKI, KIKI, MIKI, MKI, KI.

Cut off a piece of the sowing seed of the plots from the house, from the area, from the dwelling of A., the son of B., in the name of the Father, the Saviour, his Holy Son, the Holy Ghost, Amen!

And (by) the fragrance concealed in thy Name, Oh that thou would'st cause (the silence?) of the desolation to cease, and again . . . Draw out this thorn of A., son of B., by these names I bind this thorn; Jah does in no way prosper it: in the name of ΠΙΠΙ (?), Simon, Markun (Marcian), and Mani (Manes), Amen!

§ 19. ON THE EVIL EYE[2].   [Cf. A, § 23, B, § 9.]

.   .   .   .

boys and girls, the soul of cattle, the fowl of heaven; and Gabriel, the angel, said unto her: Hast thou not been up to Paradise, nor seen the Living God, Him to whom thousands upon thousands, and myriads of myriads of holy angels minister, and who sanctify his Name? You are bound by me, and I bind you, and excommunicate you, and destroy you, O Evil and Envious Eye, eye of the seven evil and envious neighbours, eye of all kinds, the eye that woundeth and pitieth not, the eye of the father, the eye of the mother[3],

---

[1] I regard my rendering of this section but as an attempt at a difficult solution. Is the original correct?

[2] I add this heading; it is wanting in the original, as are also the opening words of the Charm, to supply which see parallels in A and B.

[3] I have a strong suspicion based upon B, § 9, 100, that ܩܢ݂ܝܪ̈ܐ of

the eye of the foreigner, the eye of the gentile, (the eye of the foreigner), the dark-grey eye, the jealous eye, the caerulean eye, (the eye of those far off), the eye of all wicked men, the eye of those far off and those near, the eye of all kinds, the eye of man and woman, the eye of old men and old women, the eye of evil and envious men, the eye of the infidel, from the house, from the possessions, from the sons and daughters, from whatever else there may be to him who bears this charm, Amen!

§ 20. CONCERNING BLOOD COMING FROM THE NOSTRIL.
[*Cf*. A, § 49.]

Zachariah came to Cana; the waters dried up, and the blood dried up. Thus may the blood of A., the son of B., dry up from the nostril, Amen, Amen!

Write upon the eyes, Amen!

§ 21. BINDING THE DREAM. [*Cf*. A, § 36.]

In the name of the Father, the Son, and the Holy Ghost.

In the name of our Lord, Jesus Christ, and in the name of Mar Christopher and Mar Pityon, and the revered of yore, I bind the false dreams that are by night and day, all the phantasies of accursed evil demons that mislead, from off him who bears this charm, in the name of the Father, the Son, and Holy Ghost, Amen!

Before you begin the word of the passage ordained: 'The King hath sent,' begin, 'In the name of the Father,' Amen!

§ 22. BINDING THE SCORPION. [*Cf*. A, § 38.]

[As the text here is most corrupt, it cannot be translated as it stands. I, therefore, refer the reader to the corresponding and more correct passages in A and B.M.]

---

the MS. is a phonetic error for ܐܪܡܥܐ 'of tears', 'tearful', and this in spite of the word ܐܪܥܐ preceding, which seems to have crept in by an afterthought, suggested by ܐܪܡܥܐ.

§ 23. Binding the serpent (lit. 'sea-monster').
[*Cf.* A, § 37.]

In the name of the Father, the Son, and the Holy Ghost.

The voice of the enchanter and men wise in magic lore; the ear is stopped, that it will not hear; root out, O Lord, the teeth of the lions (!) as water that is poured out; I bind the black serpent, the red serpent, the dark-grey serpent, the silent serpent, the sea-monster, son of the sea-monster, Zargin, Zargin, Zerizin, Zargigin [1]; I bind them by Jeremiah the prophet, by Moses, and by Daniel; I bind all kinds of serpents and reptile evil and low from off the body and soul, from the children of him who carries this charm, Amen!

§ 24. Loosening the chase. [*Cf.* A, § 14.]

In the name of the Father, the Son, and the Holy Ghost.

In the same manner as God commanded the just and righteous Noah, (saying): 'Make unto thee an ark of wood, and gather therein all creeping things, all the winged fowl of heaven', so may there be gathered the birds and winged creatures of the air in front of him who bears these writs; may the spoil (of the chase) be sent from the east and from the west, from the north and from the south, from the seas, from islands, from the mountains, from the heights; from every spot may the sport be sent in the case of him who bears this charm, by the prayer of Mar Simon Peter, Andrew [2], Matthew, Mark, Luke, John, and Paul, Amen!

§ 25. The ban of Mar 'Abd-īshō', the saint.
[*Cf.* B, § 7.]

In the name of the Father, the Son, and the Holy Ghost.

The prayer and petition of Mar 'Abd-īshō', the monk and hermit of the Living God, he who dwelt forty years in the

---

[1] *Cf.* the similar expressions in A, § 19, and B.M. § 55 (Appendix).
[2] Matt. i. 18, &c.; Acts i. 13.

mountain, smitten as regards his legs, torn on the eve of
the Sabbath, the day of the Passion of our Lord, the Redeemer;
and there appeared to him the soul of the Evil Spirit in the
guise of a hateful vulgar woman, a frightful vision, and she
called him by name [1]. . . . Martlos, six; Salmios [2], seven;
Apiton, eight; Dirba, nine; Pegoga, ten; Lilita, eleven;
Malvita, twelve; Zarduch, the dissembling (or 'compelling')
demon, the strangling mother of boys and girls. Then the
holy Mar 'Abd-īshō', with a zeal divine, equipped (lit. clad)
with bond, anathema, and bar, said to her: Thou art bound
and I bind thee, I ban thee, and I destroy thee, in the name
of the God of gods, the Lord of lords, the great and glorified
King, in the name of Emanuel [3], which symbolizes (signifies)
'With us is our God', in the name of Him who formed
Adam out of the dust, in the name of Gabriel, Michael, in
the name of Azriel, in the name of Sarphiel, in the name [4] —.

§ 26. The anathema of Paradise, of avail for all
things. [*Cf.* A, § 52, B, § 5.]

In the name of the Father, the Son, and the Holy Ghost.

By the prayers of our just and righteous Fathers, Abba
Marcus, Abba Serapion, Abba Dubina, Abba Paulus, Abba
Moushé, Abba Thomis, Abba Sargis, Mar John the Evangelist,
Mar John the Baptist, Mar John Avila, Mar John Sābā, Mar
John of Herta, Mar John Tyaya, Mar John of Baka, Mar
John of Tura, Mar John of Nehila, Mar John the Seer,
Mar John of Jilu, Mar John Nahlaya, Mar John Taba, Mar
John the Teacher, Mar John Baeya, Mar John of Hetra,
Mar John of Shenna, Mar John of Dassan, Mar John of
Anzal, Mar John of Ashnu, Mar John of Naza, Mar John
of Rabana (or Cabana).

1 Part of the text is clearly omitted here; *cf.* B, § 7.
2 In B we have 'Samyos'.   3 Isa. vii. 14; viii. 8.
4 Abrupt termination.

§ 27. THE GATE OF [OR 'SECTION ON'] GRAIN [1].
[*Cf.* A, § 15.]

In the name of the Father, the Son, and the Holy Ghost.

O Lord, God Almighty, Lord of all souls and spirits that are in heaven and earth, the Creator of our father Adam, who breathed in him the breath of life, made him rule over all things, He who spake unto the just and righteous Noah, 'Prepare unto thyself an ark of wood and gather therein all things, of the creeping things, of winged creatures, of the fowl, of the cattle'; thus at the command of the Lord God, and in the name of that great Angel, chief of the holy angels, helpers, may there be gathered all the good things to the house of him who bears this charm, from every place, from every spot, from all positions, from the east, from the west, from the south, and from the north, fine provision and good fortune (lit. grain), aye and beautiful, Amen, to the house of him who bears this charm, in the name of the Living God, the Saviour, in the name of Christopher [2], Hippocrates (?) [3], and holy Susannah [4]; by that Power, great and mighty, that moveth from the heaven and the earth, may there come the good things to the house of him who bears this charm, by the Living Sign of the Cross of our Lord God, Amen, Amen. So be it!

§ 28. BINDING THE GUN OF THE WARRIORS.
[*Cf.* A, §§ 9, 16.]

In the name of the Father, the Son, and the Holy Ghost.

The voice of the Lord cutting the flame of fire; the voice of the Lord against Gog and Magog; the voice of the Lord against the craft of philosophers, against the war-implements of evil men, the profane, the foreigner, the infidel; by that Word of our Lord, Jesus Christ, do I bind the mouths of

---

[1] Perhaps also in a figurative sense: business, fortune, success.

[2] *Cf.* § 21 of this MS.   [3] ܩܠܝܣܛܘܣ (?).   [4] Luke viii. 3.

their guns, the flints, the war-instrument, the spear. May their eyes be darkened, so that they shall not see! By that Voice that cried aloud on the Cross, saying: 'My God, my God, why hast Thou forsaken me?' by that Power do I bind the guns of evil and wicked men from off him who bears this charm, by the prayer of Mar George, the triumphant martyr, Amen, Amen!

§ 29. THE GATE OF [OR 'SECTION ON'] THE WAY.

In the name of the Father, the Son, and the Holy Ghost.

The God of Abraham, the God of Isaac, the God of Jacob; the God of the just and righteous Fathers!

ܟܬܒܐ ܕܦܘܬܝܐ

ܥܠܬܐ ܕܕܝܘܢܐ

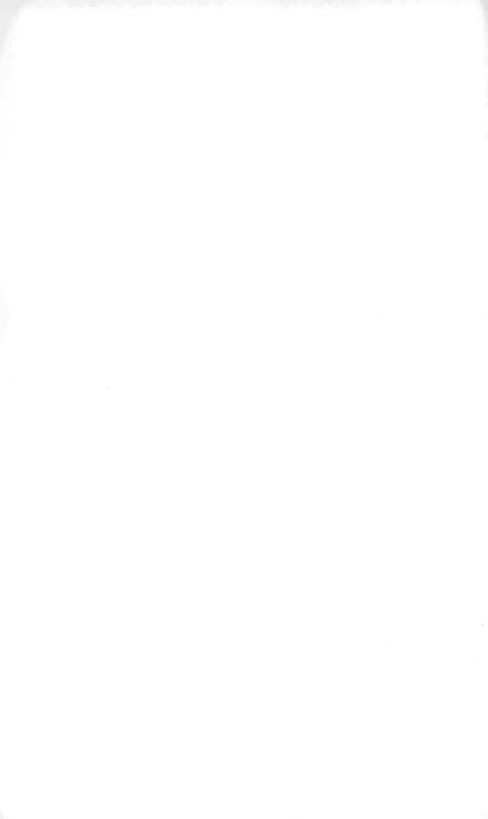

CONTENTS

CODEX A

A 2

CONTENTS

CONTENTS

CODEX B

CODEX C

CONTENTS

LIST OF ILLUSTRATIONS IN CODEX A AND B

(*Cf.* Introduction, xxi–xxii)

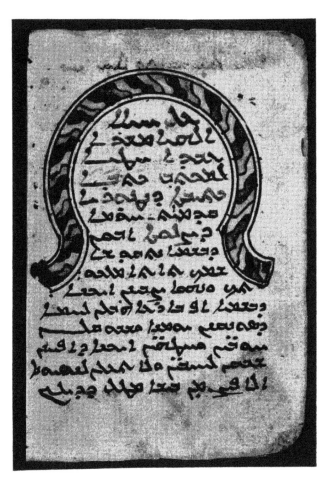

COD. A, P. 1

To face p. 1

ܥܠ ܚܝܠܐ ܐܠܗܝܐ ܡܫܪܝܐ
ܥܒܕܐ ܚܛܝܐ ܠܡܟܬܒ ܟܬܝܒܬܐ

§ 1 ܕܢܛܘܪܐ § ܘܡܕܐܟܬ ܫܪܝܐ ܕܨܠܘܬܐ

ܐܒܘܢ ܕܒܫܡܝܐ ܢܬܩܕܫ ܫܡܟ ܬܐܬܐ ܡܠܟܘܬܟ ܘܢܗܘܐ ܨܒܝܢܟ[1] ܐܝܟܢܐ ܕܒܫܡܝܐ ܐܦ ܒܐܪܥܐ ܗܒ ܠܢ ܠܚܡܐ ܕܣܘܢܩܢܢ ܝܘܡܢܐ ܘܫܒܘܩ ܠܢ ܚܘ̈ܒܝܢ ܘܚܛ̈ܗܝܢ ܐܝܟܢܐ ܕܐܦ ܚܢܢ ܫܒܩܢ ܠܚܝ̈ܒܝܢ ܘܠܐ ܬܥܠܢ ܠܢܣܝܘܢܐ ܐܠܐ ܦܨܢ ܡܢ ܒܝܫܐ ܡܛܠ ܕܕܝܠܟ ܡܠܟܘܬܐ ܚܝܠܐ ܘܬܫܒܘܚܬܐ ܠܥܠܡ ܥܠܡܝܢ

§ 2 ܨܠܘܬܐ ܕܐܕܡ

ܠܒܘܪܝܐ ܕܟܠܐ ܡܘܕܝܢ ܘܠܟ ܣܓܕ ܡܫܝܚܐ ܡܫܒܚܝܢ ܕܐܢܬ ܡܒܣܡܢܐ ܕܦ̈ܓܪܝܢ. ܘܐܢܬ ܦܪܘܩܐ ܕܢܦ̈ܫܬܢ.

§ 3 ܨܠܘܬܐ ܕܡܠܐܟ̈ܐ ܩܕ̈ܝܫܐ

ܐܠܗܐ ܩܕܝܫܐ ܚܝܠܬܢܐ ܩܕܝܫܐ ܠܐ ܡܝܘܬܐ. ܡܪܝ ܐܬܪܚܡܥܠܝܢ. ܡܪܝ ܩܒܠ ܒܥܘܬܢ. ܡܪܝ ܐܬܪܥܐ ܥܠ ܥܒܕܝܟ ܗܢܐ ܛܠܝܢ ܡܘ̈ܕܐ ܗ: ܐܡܝܢ ܘܐܡܝܢ.

[1] MS. ܨܒܝܢ.

§ 4 ܫܪ̈ܒܐ ܕܐܘܦܠܛܘܢ ܕܫܡܝܢ ܠܟܠ ܒܐܒܝ̈ܢ[1] ܘܟܠ ܒܗܘ̈ܪܡܝܢ[2]

ܒܪܫܝܬ ܐܝܬܘܗܝ, ܗ̇ܘܐ ܡܠܬܐ. ܗ̣ܘ ܡܠܬܐ ܐܝܬܘܗܝ,
ܗܘܐ ܠܘܬ ܐܠܗܐ ܘܐܠܗܐ ܐܝܬܘܗܝ, ܗܘܐ ܗ̣ܘ[3]
ܡܠܬܐ ܗܢܐ ܐܝܬܘܗܝ, ܗܘܐ ܒܪܫܝܬ ܠܘܬ ܐܠܗܐ
ܟܠ ܒܐܝܕܗ ܗ̣ܘܐ ܘܒܠܥܕܘܗܝ, ܐܦܠܐ ܚܕܐ ܗܘܬ

ܡܕܡ	ܕܗܘܐ	ܒܗ	ܚ̈ܝܐ	ܗܘܐ	ܘܚ̈ܝܐ
ܐܝܬ	ܝܗܘܢ	ܢܘܗ	ܪ̇ܐ	ܕܒܢ̈ܝ	ܐܢ̄ܫܐ
ܗ̣ܘ	ܢܘܗ	ܪ̇ܐ	ܒܚܫ	ܘܟܐ	ܠܐ
ܐܕܪ-	ܟܗ	ܒܚܝܠܐ	ܕܗܠܝܢ	ܒܫܡ̇ܪ	ܐ
ܩ̈ܛܠ	ܡܟܐ	ܡܪ̈-	ܢܝܐ	ܘܐܠ-	ܗ̈ܝܐ
ܘܒ-	ܫܡ	ܐܗ	ܢ̇ܝ	ܐܣܪ̇	ܗܢ̇ܝ

[1] MS. ܒܐܒܝܢ. [2] MS. ܒܗܘܪܡܝܢ.
[3] MS. ܗ̇ܘܐ (*cf.* John i. 1-5).

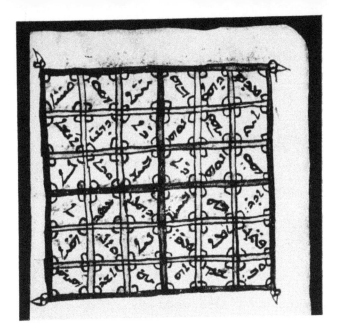

Cod. A, p. 3

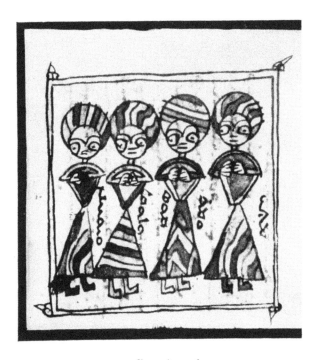

Cod. A, p. 4

To face p. 3

ܐܝܒܐ ܕܚܕܝ ܝܒܝܪܐ ܠܐܦܝܠܘ ܩܣܐܝܟܘ ܕܐܝܒܝܫ ᴑ $\S\,5$
---

[1] Shortened for ܩܐܝܕ݂ܝܣܐ.

[2] Abbreviation for ܕܠܬ݂ܒ ܣܪܐܝ ܗܠܡ.

ܩ̈ܘ: ܗ: ܐܬܚܫܒܬ ܠܗ ܘܒܗܘܬܐ ܠܒܪ ܕܐ̈ܪܡ ܘܒܕܡܐ
ܠܟܠܗ ܒܝ̈ܠܕܬܐ ܕܒܪܬܗ، ܡܪܝܡ ܦܬܟܢܬܐ ܘܕܡܪܝ،
ܘܗܫܐ ܡܒܕܡܕܢܐ ܐܡܝܢ

§ 6 ܕܦܘܡ ܫܡ̈ܠܠܝܐ

ܒܫܡ ܐܒܐ ܘܒܪܐ ܘܪܘ: ܕܩܘ: ܐܒܐ ܠܟܬܒܐ
ܒܫܐܠܬ ܘܒܪܐ ܕܦܘܦܪܝܐ ܠܡܐܠܬ ܘܪܘܚܢܐ ܕܡܘܕܥܢܐ
ܒܡܪܐ ܒܝ ܐܣܝܠܐܝܬ ܡܢ ܒܢܝܐ ܠܐ ܠܐ ܕܚܠ ܐܢܐ
ܐܡܢܢܐܝܬ ܘܟܠ ܒܢܝܢܐ ܕܡܡܪܚ ܘܫܐܪ ܒܟ:
ܩ̈ܘ: ܗ: ܐܫܪܢܐ ܠܗ ܘܡܫܪܒܢܐ ܠܗ ܒܗ، ܡܠܬܐ
ܕܐܡܪ ܡܪܢ ܠܬܠܡܝ̈ܕܘܗܝ، ܘܟܠ ܡܕܡ ܕܬܐܫܪܘܢ
ܒܐܪܥܐ ܢܗܘܐ ܐܫܝܪ ܒܫܡܝܐ ܗܟܢܐ ܡܪܝܐ
ܐܠܗܐ ܚܝܠܬܢܐ ܐܫܪܝܐ ܦܓ̈ܪܐ ܘܠܒ̈ܝܐ ܕܥܠܡܘܢ
ܒܢ̈ܝܢܐ ܒܢ̈ܝܐ ܘܒܢ̈ܬܐ ܘܓܒ̈ܪܐ ܘܢܫ̈ܐ ܘܥܠ̈ܝܡܐ
ܘܥܠܝ̈ܡܬܐ ܘܣ̈ܒܐ ܘܐܡܗ̈ܬܐ ܘܫܒ̈ܘܩܬܐ (?) ܘܓ̈ܪܒܐ
ܡܢ ܟܠ: ܩ̈ܘ: ܗ: ܒܗ̇ܘ ܚܝܠܐ ܘܒܗ̇ܘ ܠܒܢܝܢܐ ܕܠܒܫ
ܗܘܐ ܐܠܟܣܢܕܪܘܣ ܒܪ ܦܝܠܝܦܘܣ ܒܗ ܒܒܝܬܐ ܟܠܗ̇
ܐܪܥܐ ܗܟܢܐ ܡܪܝܐ ܐܠܗܐ ܚܝܠܬܢܐ ܢܬܒܢܐ ܓܒܗ
ܕܟܠܗܘܢ ܒܢܝ̈ܢܐ ܒܢ̈ܝܐ ܡܢܡ ܟܠ: ܩ̈ܘ: ܗ: ܒܫܘܦܐ
ܕܫܘܒܚܐ ܘܒܬܫ̈ܒܚܬܐ ܕܒܠܗ ܐܡܝܢ. ܡܪܝܐ ܐܠܗܐ
ܚܝܠܬܢܐ ܐܝܟ ܕܐܦܩܬ ܠܝܘܣܦ ܡܢ ܒܝܬ ܐܣܝ̈ܪܐ
ܘܦܨܝܬ ܠܕܘܝܕ ܡܢ ܐܝ̈ܕܝ ܫܐܘܠ ܡܠܟܐ ܘܫܘܙܒܬ
ܠܕܘܝܕ ܡܢ ܓܐܘܠ ܘܦܨܝܬ ܠܐܠܝܐ ܡܢ ܐܚܐܒ ܘܠܕܢܝܐܝܠ
ܚܢܢܝܐ ܡܢ ܐܬܘܢܐ ܕܢܘܪܐ ܘܠܕܢܝܐܝܠ ܡܢ ܒܒ̈ܠܝܐ.
ܗܟܢܐ ܡܪܝܐ ܐܠܗܐ ܚܝܠܬܢܐ ܕܬܫܘܙܒ ܠܗ
ܠܥܒܕܟ[1] ܗܢܐ ܡܢ ܟܠ: ܩ̈ܘ: ܗ: ܐܦ̈ܝܐ ܠܝ̈ܠܝܬܐ

[1] I have added the ܠ.

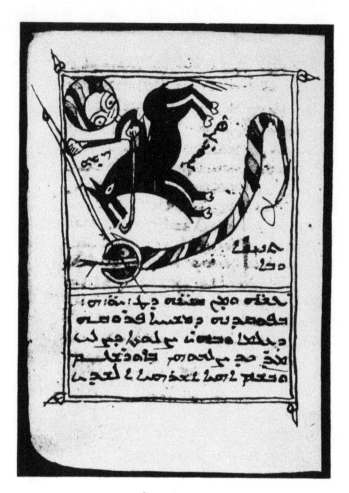

Cod. A, p. 6

To face p. 4

---

[1] Shortened for ܐܢܪܝܣܝܐ. [2] MS. ܐܕܝܟܒܪܣ.

[3] MS. ܐܪܐܒܪܐ.

ܪ̇ܘܚܐ ܘܐܚܘܕ ܫܦܝܐ ܒܝܡܝܢܗ ܘܩܫܬܐ ܒܣܡܠܗ
ܘܢܬܬܪܣܩ ܓܫܡܗ ܩܕܡ ܡܠܟ̈ܐ ܘܫܠܝܛܢ̈ܐ ܘܐܡܝܢ̈ܐ
ܘܕ̈ܝܢܐ ܘܫܠܝܛܢ̈ܐ ܘܢܬܠܦܦ ܒܠܒܘܫܗ ܐܝܟ ܕܢܨܚ
ܫܘܦܪܗ ܕܡܘܫܐ ܒܒ̈ܢܝ ܝܣܪܝܠ ܗܟܢܐ ܢܨܚ ܫܘܦܪܗ
ܕܝܠܗ: ܬ̈ܘ: ܩܕܡ ܡܠܟ̈ܐ ܘܫܠܝܛܢ̈ܐ ܘܡܕܒܪ̈ܢܐ ܘܕ̈ܝܢܐ
ܐܝܟ ܛܠܝܐ ܕܦܪܥܘܢ ܩܕܡ ܝܘܣܦ ܗܟܢܐ ܢܣܓܕܘܢ
ܠܗ ܒܬܠܬ̈ܝܐ ܘܡܫܡ̈ܫܢܐ ܘܐܢܫܐ ܒܢ̈ܝܐ ܘܕ̈ܝܢܝܐ
ܘܫܠܝܛܢ̈ܐ ܘܦܠܛܘܪ̈ܐ ܕܝܢ ܠܝ: ܬܘ: ܗ: ܒܝܠܘܬ ܡܪܬܝ،
ܡܪ̇ܝܡ ܬܫܒܘܚܬܐ ܐܡܝܢ

ܐܝܟ ܕܐܙܠ ܠܘܬ ܕܪ̈ܝܐ §8

ܒܬܪ ܐܝܟܐ ܘܟܕ ܐܬܐ ܘܐܘܪܫܐ ܕܝܘ: ܦܕܪܐ ܕܪ̈ܝܐ ܘܦܠܚܐ
ܘܫܦܪܬܗ ܘܫܝܢܬܗ ܠܕ̇ܝܢܐ ܘܠܚܒܘܫܬܐ ܢܦܩܘ ܠܗ
ܒܠܫܘܕ̈ܘܗܝ، ܗܕܝܢܐ ܒܓܪܫ ܡܠܐܟܐ ܕܝܢ ܡܫܝܚ[1]
ܕ̈ܘܟܐ ܕܝܢ ܫܡܠܝ[2] ܘܡܪܘܦ ܒܠܝ ܘܡܬܠܦܪ ܠܝ ܥܡ
ܐܗܝ̇ܗ ܐܫܪܗܝܐ ܐܠܫܕܝ، ܐܕܘܢܝ ܡܪܝܐ ܨܒܐܘܬ
ܐܫܪܗܝܐ ܬܘܩܦܐ ܘܗܕܝܪܐ ܒܫܘܒܚܐ ܕܩܐܡ ܠܟܠ
ܕܝܢ ܪܫܝ[3] ܘܡܬܠܦܪ ܠܝ ܕܝܢ ܒܠܗܘܢ ܒܒܥܠܕܒ̈ܒܝ ܫܟܝ
ܘܡܡܟܝܢ ܠܟܠܗܘܢ ܐܝܠܝܢ ܕܡܬܬܪ̇ܡܝܢ ܥܠܝ ܬܫܒܘܚܬܝ،
ܘܐܝܠܝܢ ܕܢܬܒܥܝܢ ܩܕܡܝ ܘܫܕܪ، ܢܗܘܘܢ ܠܝ[4] ܡܥܕ̈ܕ[5]
ܘܡܫܡ̈ܫܢܐ ܘܡܬܠܦ̈ܪܢܐ ܘܐܝܟ ܟܠܒܐ ܢܡܠܚܘܢܝ
ܘܐܝܟ ܛܠܝܐ ܢܫܡܫܘܢܝ ܒܪ̈ܫܝܗܘܢ ܒܫܡܗ ܕܡܠܟܐ
ܡܫܝܚܐ ܕܐܢ ܒܠܗܘܢ ܒܒܥܠܕܒ̈ܒܝ ܕܝܢ ܗܫܐ ܠܝ
ܡܕܝܢܐ ܐܘܢ[6] ܕܒܡܫܝܚܐ ܗܘ، ܒܟܡܐ ܘܬܐ ܠܐܝܠܝ

[1] MS. ܡܫܝܚܗ.
[2] MS. ܫܡܠܗ.
[3] MS. ܗܫܪ.
[4] MS. ܠܗ.
[5] Shortened for ܒܥܠܕܒ̈ܒܐ.
[6] *Sic*, evidently ܐܒܘܢ.

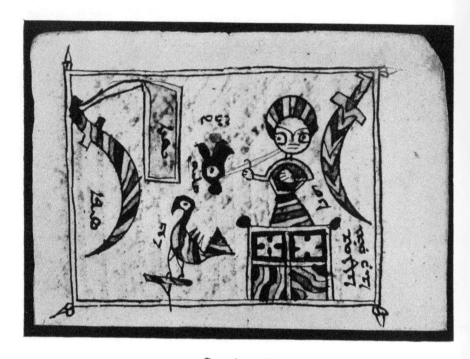

COD. A, P. 11

To face p. 6

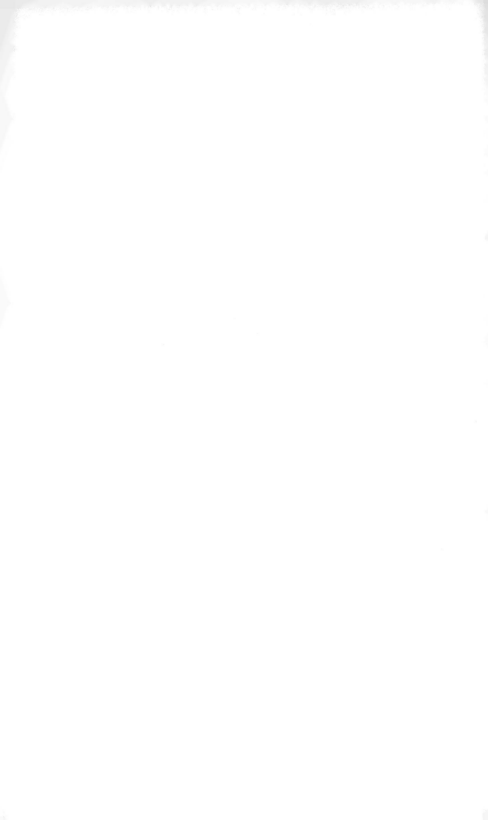

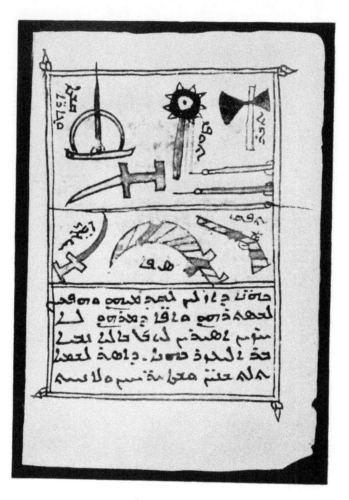

COD. A, P. 15

CODEX A

Syriac text page.

ܥܘܪ ܠܥܠ ܒܝܢ ܐܠܐ ܘܐܝܬ ܠܒܝܢ ܡܕܝܢܬܗ ܠܠܐܒܐ
ܘܡܢ ܐܪܝܟ ܕܒܝܪ ܐܒܟܡܢܐ ܕܗܢܝ ܐܝܟ ܕܝܪܘܚܬܐ
ܘܢܚܬܐ ܒܝܢ ܩܕܡܝܐ ܘܐܝܪܐ ܒܝܢ ܩܕܡܐ ܘܡܚܒܐ
ܘܗܠܝܢ : ܬܢ : ܠ ܡܪܝ ܒܝܢ ܘܐܬܟܬܐܦܘܢ ܘܬܚܘܝܢܐ
ܐܪܝܟܘܢ ܘܡܚܒܘܝܗܘܢ ܘܢܚܬܪܝܗܘܢ ܘܩܒܘܗܝܢ
ܘܗܢܘܬܐ ܐܬܢ ܚܬܐ ܠܠܥܐ ܘܩܕܡܐ ܡܢ ܠܟܠ ܡܒܝܕܐ، ܒܝܪܝ
ܐܡܪܝܢ ܠܒܩܬܐ

§ 10 ܣܘܪܐ ܕܐܝܬܘܗܝ ܐܟܒܠܐ

ܕܡܫܚ ܠܩܘܡܐ ܘܠܝܚ

ܐܡܪ ܐܠܐ ܘܐܝܢ ܒܝܢܐ : ܘܒܢ : ܘܒܢܐ ܐܡܪܘܗܝ
ܐܟܒܠܐ ܕܒܢܝܐ ܕܒܝܢ ܐܝܟܪ، ܐܝܟ ܐܬܚܙܝܪܗ
ܐܟܒܠܐ : ܒܝܢ ܐܬܐ ܠܒܫܪܐ ܚܬܐ ܒܝܢ ܘܒܢܘܩܒܐ
ܘܐܬܐ ܘܐܒܗ ܠ ܕܕ ܠܗ ܒܚܒܝܢ ܘܐܬܐ
ܘܩܕܡ ܩܘܪܐ ܚܒܣܝ ܡܚܝ ܟܚܒܣܐ ܘܐܬܘܐ
ܘܠܐ ܒܝܢ : ܘܡܟܠܠ ܒܝܢ ܐܝܪܐ ܘܪܒܝܢ ܘܠܐ
ܡܘܢ ܒܪ ܐܟܒܠܠ ܠܗ ܐܡܪ ܗܘܐ ܘܕܠܓܐ ܗܢ
ܒܝܢ ܒܝܢ ܘܗܬ ܘܗܢܘܬܦ ܐܡܪܝܢ

§ 11 ܕܒܠ ܚܠ ܘܩܒܘܗܝ

ܐܡܪ ܐܠܐ ܘܐܝܢ ܒܝܢܐ : ܘܩܘܡܒܐ ܒܣܘܕ ܪܒܐ
ܘܚܬܪܐ ܘܚܬܐ ܕܐܟܒܠܐ ܠܐܟܠܐ ܕܪܝܢܒܐ ܚܝܢ ܘܚܬܐ
ܘܢܝ ܐܪܬܐ ܕܬܚ ܒܡܚܒܪܐ ܘܒܝܬܐ ܒܣܡܗ ܐܪܫܒܐ
ܐܟܪܝܘܐ ܘܐܬܪܘܐ ܠ ܠܝܕܢܘܒܕܘܝܐ ܘܟܠܪܐ ܘܐܬ،
ܐܡ ܡܬܚܒܬܗܝ، ܠܠ ܚܬܐ ܚܒܐ ܘܩܕܝܐ ܐܬܬܗ ܐܟܒܐ
ܘܐܟܒܐ ܐܬܬܗܕܬ ܚܒܝܗܝ ܘܒܒܘܪܐ ܐܒܪ ܬܚܬ ܐܬܐ
ܘܐܟܒܘܩܘ ܐܟܪܐ ܘܢܒܝܐ ܘܚܠܘܐ ܘܩܒܠܐ

ܢܘܡܝܗ ܠܗܩ ܐܪܒ ܠܗܩ ܚܝܠܐ ܘܐܒܪ ܐܪܙ ܘܐܒܪ
ܐܠܝܢ ܂ܕܒܬܠܬܗܡܕ ܐܠܠܗܟ ܐܡܝܚܕ ܚܒ ܂ܕܪܝܬ ܐܒܪܘܬ ܣܒܗܘܝܝ
ܐܠܗܪ ܐܝܪܘܬܐ ܡܟ ܦܡ ܂ܕܐܝܩܪ ܐܠܗܪ ܠܐܣܐܝܕܢ ܡܬܒܘ
ܐܪܕܝ ܐܝܠܐ ܗܡ ܥܠ ܐܠܗܩܕܝܝܢܕ ܐܝܡܢ ܐܘܪܝܢܐ
ܟܬܒܝܠܬ ܐܘܪ ܐܘܡܠܐ ܡܪܒ ܡܣܒܢ ܐܪܐܙ̈
ܐܠܗܒܕ ܚܝܪܒܢ ܗܡܠ ܕܒܠܘܐܪ ܐܒܡܕ ܬܠܝܬܠ
ܐܝܪܟܐ ܐܝܪܘܡܩ ܐܝܚ ܝܠܗܣܩ ܝܚܩܣܡ ܪܡܝܕ ܐܝܚܣ
ܐܝܠܗ̇ܠ ܚܒܕܟܙܩ ܣܥܙܪܒܠܕ ܐܝܠܒ ܂ܙ ܠܒܙܕ ܐܝܒܚ
ܐܝܘܚܩ ܐܒܙܝ ܐܝܠܙ ܐܘܡܩ ܐܝܒܪ ܥܠܒܕ ܐܠܐܚ̈ܘܡܩ
ܝܙܬܩ ܐܠܗܘܢ̈ܬܠ ܐܝܠܚ ܗܡ ܢܝܟ ܦܝܚܒ ܐܝܡܩ ܐܪܩ
ܡܒ ܐܗܘܪܚܒ ܂ܡ ܂ܐܗ̈ ܂ܠ̇ ܐܝܡܩ ܝܒܪܕܠ ܝܪܝܪܒܥ
ܚܒܠܓܒ ܐܗܡܒ̈ܚ ܐܝܪܘ̈ ܐܝܡܪܒܣܩ ܐܗܪ̈ܐ ܢܘܡܠܒ
ܦܪܒܐܪ ܐܝܪܘܪ̈ ܢܘܡܠܒ

---

§ 12 ܚܝܪܐ ܕܐܝܕܝ̈ܐ ܂ܕܗܘܬܡܣܡܩ ܢܒܝܫܩ

ܐܝܠܘܐܢ ܕܒܪܝܕ ܚܝܪܐ ܡܩܝܗ̈

ܒܥܡ ܐܪܐ ܐܒܝܩ ܐܝܐ ܂ ܐܝܒ ܂ ܐܠܩܒ ܂ ܐܬܚܒܣܡܗ ܐܒܝܩܐܘܩܗ
ܐܘ̈ܒܪ (!) ܓܒܠܝܐ̈ܒܝ ܂ܕܒܪܝܕ ܐܬܚܝܝܢܚܗ ܐܬܚܒܣܚܗ
ܝܢܝܒ ܝܪܒܣܡ ܐܠܒܒܩ ܐܘܡ ܐܝܪܒܕ ܗܡܐ ܐ̈ܝܒ
ܐܠܓܘ ܢܘܡܝܒ ܐܘܡ ܐܝܪܕ ܐܒܣܐܘܩ ܂ܐܝܠܟܝܒܪ ܐܬܘܒ̈ܪܐܩ
ܝܟܝܡ ܐܝܠܒ ܐܝܠܚ̈ ܐܠܡܩ ܐܝܪܒ ܐܝܪܐܩ
ܐܣܒܕܩ ܐܠܗܚܒ ܝܝܡ ܐܝܠܪܒܣܩ ܝܟܒܝܠܬܠ ܐܝܒܒܫܚܒܩ
ܐܘ̈ܒܪܝ ܚܠܒܒ ܐܗܪ̈ܐܠܒ ܒܝ ܒܝܒܓܠܘ ܥܘܠܗܩܣܩ ܥܘܝܒܦ
ܐܪܒܣܐܬܠܬܚ ܡܒ ܝܠܒ ܐܝܒܘܐܪ ܐܝܒܩ ܕܒܝܪܕ ܐܒܝܚ̈ܒ
ܠܒ ܂ܚܝܒܘܐܪ ܂ܡ ܂ܐܗ̈ ܂ܠܒ̇ ܐܝ̈ܗܡܩ ܐܒܚܒܩ ܦܚܒܩ
ܝܪܠܒܝܠܙ ܐܠܩ ܐܝܒܣ ܕܒܝܪܕ ܐܒܚܒܒܣ ܐܘ̈ܒܪܝ ܐܘ

ܟ̈ܪܒܪ ܟܡܘ̈ܩܘܕ $ 13

---

¹ In the MS. the words ܟܪ̈ܘܐ ܟ̈ܝܠ̈ܝܚܘ are added and deleted.

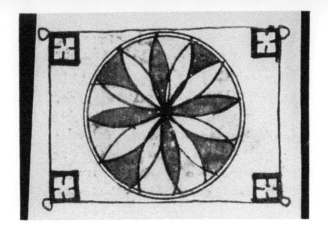

COD. A. P. 17

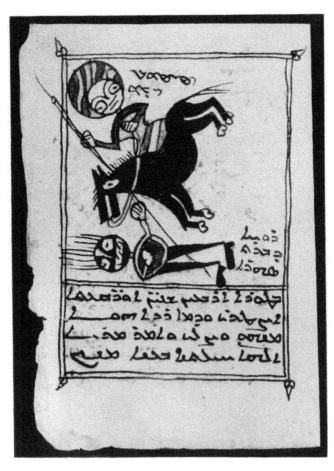

COD. A, P. 20

---

1 MS. ܝ̈ܝܡܪ.ܪ.   2 MS. *sic. Cf.* Ezek. xxxviii. 6; xxvii. 14.

3 MS. ܐܪ̈ܩܝܪ.

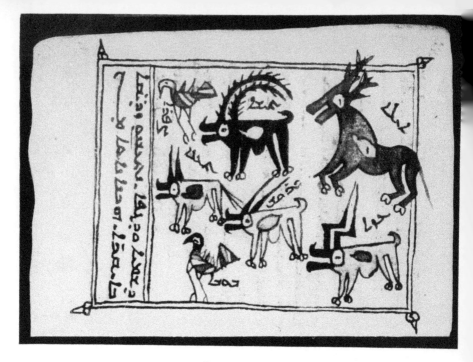

Cod. A, p. 24

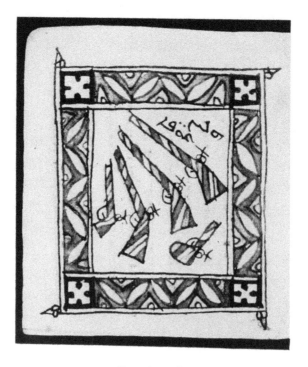

Cod. A, p. 27

To face p. 12

---

[1] Add ܐܘܪ omitted in MS.

ܚܒܗܝ ܘܒܩܣ ܚܝܠܒ ܕܝ ܒܡ : ܬܢ : ܝܒ ܟ : ܡ : ܐܡܪ   (See Appendix)

ܘܟܠܗܘܢ ܣܗ̈ܕܘܗܝ܆ ܐܝܟ ܐܡܪܬ ܕܒܢ̈ܝܐ ܡܢ ܦܘܡܐ
ܘܒܪܐ ܢܦܠ ܡܢ ܐܡܗ ܒܥܠ ܠܓܒܪܘܬܗ ܕܡܪܢ
ܘܦܠܦܠܘ[1] ܬܠܬܐ ܫܒܘ̈ܥ܆ ܗ̣ܘ܇ ܒܫܡܗ ܕܡܪܢܝܫܘܥ
ܡܫܝܚܐ ܘܐܣܝܪܐ ܠܫܡܗ ܕܡܪܬܝ܆ ܡܪܝܡ ܠܒܬܘܠܬܐ
ܘܐܣܝܪܐ ܠܫܡܗ ܕܓܒܪܝܠ ܪܝܫ ܡܠܐܟ̈ܐ ܘܡܫܝܚ܇
ܠܪܘܚܐ ܕܠܒܗ ܕܦ: ܬܘ: ܗܠܝܢ ܚ̈ܝܠܘܬ ܡܪܝ܆ ܐܘܟܝܡ
ܠܥܠܡܐ ܐܡܝܢ

ܐܣܘܪܐ ܕܦܘܡܐ ܕܟܠ̈ܒܐ § 21

ܒܫܡ ܐܒܐ ܘܒܪܐ ܘܪܘ: ܕܡܘܕܝܢܐ ܒܪܒܘܬܐ ܕܕܪ̈ܝܢ
ܬܫܒܚܬܗܘܢ ܐܝܟ ܟ̈ܐܦܐ ܫܬܩ ܐܢܘܢ ܡܪܝܐ ܐܠܗܐ
ܫܬܩ ܐܢܘܢ ܒܗܘ ܟܐܦܐ ܕܡܫܝܚܐ ܗܘܬ ܥܠ ܦܘܡ
ܡܥܪ̈ܬܗ ܕܦܪܘܩܢ ܒܗ ܢܫܬܬܩܘܢ ܟܠܒ̈ܐ ܗܠܝܢ ܚ̈ܝܠܘܬܗ[2]
ܕܡܪܬܝ܆ ܡܪܝܡ ܠܒܬܘܠܬܐ ܘܕܡܪܝ܆ ܝܘܚܢܢ ܡܥܡܕܢܐ
ܚ̈ܝܠܘܬ ܟܠܗܘܢ ܣܗ̈ܕܘܗܝ܆ ܘܩܕ̈ܝܫܘܗܝ܆ ܕܡܪܢ ܐܡܝܢ
ܒܪܝܟ ܥܠ ܬܠܬܐ ܒܢ̈ܝܐ ܘܫܒ܇ ܠܡܕܡ ܟܠܒ̈ܐ

ܐܣܘܪܐ ܕܚܠܡܐ ܒܝܫܐ § 22

ܒܫܡ ܐܒܐ ܘܒܪܐ ܘܪܘ: ܕܡܘܕܝܢܐ ܐܚܝܕ ܡܘܒܕܢܐ
ܒܒܪܗ ܕܐܠܗܐ ܪܒܐ ܗܘܐ ܒܢ̈ܝܐ ܒܝܢܬ ܫܒܒܐ
ܠܦܪ̈ܐ ܘܦܠܛ ܒܗ ܬܠܬܐ ܦܪ̈ܨܘܦ ܒܢ̈ܝܐ ܗ̣ܘ ܒܪܢܫܐ
ܒܢ̈ܝܐ ܕܐܒܐ ܒܢ̈ܝܐ ܘܐܪܝܐ ܒܢ̈ܝܐ ܒܫܡ ܐܒܐ
ܐܣܪ ܠܗ ܒܪܢܫܐ ܒܢ̈ܝܐ ܒܫܡ ܒܪܐ ܐܣܪ ܠܗ ܕܐܒܐ
ܒܢ̈ܝܐ ܒܫܡ ܪܘܚܐ ܕܩܘ: ܐܣܪ ܠܗ ܐܪܝܐ ܒܢ̈ܝܐ ܕܠܐ
ܢܬܩܪܒܘܢ ܠܦܓܪܗ ܘܠܐ ܠܒܝܬܗ ܕܦ: ܬܘ: ܗܠܝܢ
ܚ̈ܝܠܘܬ ܡܪܝܡ ܒܬܘܠܬܐ ܐܡܝܢ

[1] Delete final ܘ.
[2] This word is repeated in MS.

---

1 *Vide* Translation and Appendix.   2 MS. ܟܝܢܐ.

ܒܪ ܐܝܟܐ ܕܐܝܬ ܫܘܠܛܢܐ ܕܫܠܝܛ ܐܝܟܐ ܕܒܪ
ܬܫܬܘܪܬܗ ܥܡ ܒܢܝ ܐܢܬܬܗ ܡܢ ܪܚܡ ܗܘܐ ܒܢܝܗ ܒ ܗ:
ܘܡܗܘܐ ܠܘܩܒܠ ܗܘ ܩܕܡܘܗܝ ܘܩܝܡ ܚܠܝܨܐ ܐܡܗ: ܘܒܗ:
ܘܗܘܐ ܒܢܝܐ ܘܒܘܙܩܐ ܬܚܘܝܬܐ ܕܥܒܕܝ ܚܝܠ ܒܝܬܗ,
ܐܡܪ ܐܠܗܝܐ ܗܘܐ: ܣܘܝܢ ܟܝܬܗܐ ܓܠܝܬܐ ܐܡܪ

ܐܡܪܐ ܕܝܢ ܓܠܝܒ ܕܩܡܬܗ   § 25

ܒܕܪ ܐܡܪ ܐܪܐ ܘܒܪ ܐܝܐ: ܒܩܐ: ܒܝܬܐ ܐܬܟ
ܕܒܘܝܬܐ ܚܝܬܐ ܠܒܪ ܪܘ ܐܡܪ ܐܡܪ ܠܕܝܐ ܕܐܒܢ ܕܪܝܐ
ܕܒܪ ܒܪ ܒܪ ܒܝܢ ܚܬܠܬܐ ܘܒܬܘܕܗܐ ܕܒܘܝܬܐ
ܘܟܬܡ ܬܚܠ ܝܕ ܒܪܝ ܣܒܐ ܚܒܐ ܣܘ ܒܪ ܒܝܠܓܘ
ܐܡܪ ܒܪ ܘܒܘܝܬܐ ܘܡܣܡܒܬܐ ܙ: ܚ: ܗ: ܛ: ܡ: ܗ: ܐܡܪ

ܒܩܒܬܐ ܕܓܘܪܐ ܕܝܢ ܒܘܝܝܐ   § 26

ܒܕܪ ܐܡܪ ܐܪܐ ܘܒܪ ܐܝܐ: ܒܩܐ: ܗܠܘ ܒܪ ܚܠ ܠܒܪ
ܩܠܝܐ ܠܗ ܒܠܠ ܗܕ ܘܪܒܝܬܐ ܚܡܝܬܐ ܕܐܪܝܡܣܡ ܪܡܣܪ
ܘܐܪܘܝ ܒܕܝ ܒܪ ܡܢ ܬܚܐܠ ܘܢܟܠܝܒܘܡ, ܣܘܒܟܠܝܣܡ,
ܠܒܠ ܐܡܗ ܟܘ ܥܠܗ ܚܝܘܐ ܚܕܘܐ ܠܐ ܬܬܕܪܝ ܒܪ ܠܬܪܘܡ
ܠܐܐ ܘܠܐ ܒܪܝ ܘܠܐ ܠܐ ܠܠܠ ܒܕ ܐܬܝܪ ܠܠܒܠܘܪ ܪܣ ܘܡܕܐ ܒ:
ܠܐ ܒܕ ܠܐ ܠܠܘ ܘܠܐ ܡܘܪܟܝ ܘܠܐ ܡܘܬܒܢܝ ܪܒܐ: ܗ: ܚ:
ܠܐ ܘܠܐ ܒܬܝ ܘܠܐ ܘܠܐ ܒܪ ܡܠܝ ܘܠܐ ܚܒܝܐ ܘܠܐ
ܒܘܝܙܢܐ ܚܘܬܐ [1]ܒܒܬܐ ܒܕ ܚܬܡ ܘܡܕ ܒܪ ܣܬܘܡ
ܘܣܘܪ ܡܣܒܪ ܘܠܐ ܐܬܝܪ ܐ: ܗ: ܚ: ܛ: ܒܩܘܣ
ܘܒܘܣܣ ܘܣܓܟܐ ܘܪܚܐ ܘܢܝܐ ܘܒܪܝܣܐ ܘܚܕܝܒܬܐ
ܘܬܘ ܚܝܠܬܐ ܕܪܘܡܝܐ ܚܬܡ ܪܝܣ ܕܬܐܠܦܘ ܐܐܐܪ
ܘܥܐܪ ܘܚܒܬܐ ܠܐܬܝܠ ܒܪ ܗܘܕܘܬܗ, ܘܒܪ ܡܗܒܢܐ:
ܐܡܪ: ܒ: ܕ: ܒ:

<hr />

[1] I have added ܠ.

§ 27 ܚܪܡܐ ܕܪܒܢ ܗܘܪܡܝܙܕ ܕܢܥܫ ܠܟܠܒ̈ܐ ܦܩܪ̈ܐ

ܒܫܡ ܐܒܐ ܘܒܪܐ ܘܪܘܚܐ ܕܩܘ: ܝܠܕܘܬܗ ܘܥܡܕܬܗ
ܘܨܠܝܒܘܬܗ ܘܩܝܡܬܗ ܕܡܪܝ، ܪܒܢ ܗܘܪܡܝܙܕ ܕܦܪ̈ܣܝܐ
ܒܪܗ ܕܝܘܣܦ ܪܫܝܢܐ ܕܝܠܗ ܘܡܚܒܐ ܡܢ ܐܠܗܐ
ܪܘܚܢܝܐ ܘܡܪܘܡܡܢܐ ܒܛܒܢܐ ܕܟܘܠܠܗ ܘܐܡܪ ܡܪܝܐ
ܐܠܗܐ ܚܠܝܬܐ ܒܒܢܐ ܡܢܝ ܘܡܬܒܥܒܥܐ ܠܦܘܡܗܘܢ
ܟܠܗܘܢ ܕܢܬܚܙܘܢ ܥܡܗܝܢ ܦܬܓܡܐ ܘܥܡܗ ܕܟܠ ܒܒܢܝܢ
ܗܘܪܡܝܙܕ ܕܚܟܝܡܐ ܠܐ ܢܟܬ ܘܢܟܬ ܠܗ ܟܠܒܐ
ܦܩܪܐ ܘܐܪܝܐ ܡܚܒܠܢܐ ܘܢܡܪܐ ܡܪܝܪܐ ܘܚܝܘܬܐ
ܘܕܐܒܐ ܒܡܐܟܠܢܐ ܘܟܠܗܝܢ ܚܝ̈ܘܬܐ ܡܙܝܩܢܝܬܐ ܡܢܗ
ܘܡܢ ܒܢܝܗ ܘܡܢ ܒܢܘ̈ܗܝ، ܘܡܢ ܒܢܝܗ ܘܡܢ ܟܠܡܕܡ
ܕܐܝܬ ܠܗ ܘܕܗܘܐ ܠܗ ܠܥ: ܐ̈ܡ: ܗ: ܒܝܠܘܬ ܡܪܬܝ،
ܡܪܝܡ ܝܠܕܬܐܠܗܐ ܐܡܝܢ

§ 28 ܐܣܘܪܐ ܕܐܫܬܐ

ܒܫܡ ܐܒܐ ܘܒܪܐ ܘܪܘ: ܕܩܘܕܫܐ ܡܪܝ: ܚܝ ܡܪܝ:
ܐܝܟܠܠ ܡܪܝ ܡܚܝܬ ܡܪܝ: ܡܢ ܬܬܦܣܢ ܘܬܬܦܣܘܢܐ
ܘܬܬܦܠܓܐ ܐܫܬܐ ܚܡܝܡܬܐ ܘܩܪܝܪܬܐ ܘܒܪܘܝܬܐ
ܘܡܗܘܕܝܬܐ ܘܟܠ ܟܢܫ ܕܐܫܬܐ ܡܢ ܦܓܪܗ ܘܡܢ
ܢܦܫܗ ܕܦ: ܒ: ܕܦ: ܐܡܝܢ ܕܪܫܝܡܐ ܡܕܝܢܐ ܡܢ
ܡܪ̈ܒܐ ܘܠܪ̈ܒܢܐ ܡܢ ܬܫܡܫܬܐ ܘܬܒܪܘܡ ܘܬܪܫܡ
ܐܫܬܐ ܚܡܝܡܬܐ ܘܩܪܝܪܬܐ ܘܒܪܘܝܬܐ ܘܟܠܟܢܫ
ܕܐܫܬܐ ܡܢ ܦܓܪܗ ܘܡܢ ܢܦܫܗ ܕܦ: ܡܗ: ܗ: ܐܡܝܢ
ܘܐܡܝܢ

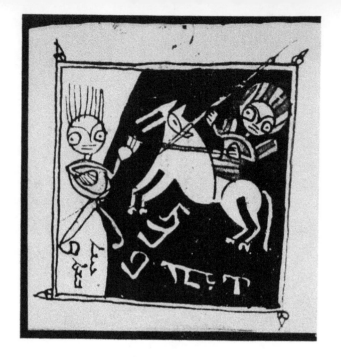

Cod. A, p. 34

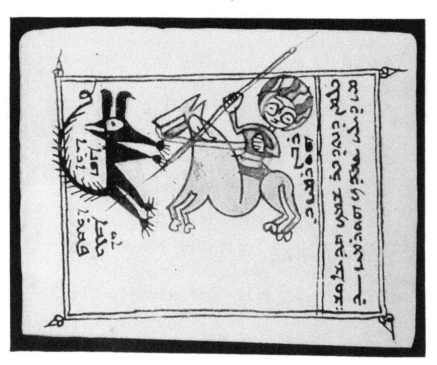

Cod. A, p. 39

To face p. 18

ܒܝܬܗ ܒܪ. ܫܦܝܘ ܘܢܗܦܘܟ ܒܪ. ܠܓܒܝܢ ܘܬܐܬܐ
ܡܒܡܠܬܗ ܚܕ. ܒܬܠܬܝܢ ܘܒܫܬܝܢ ܘܒܡܐܐ ܬܗܘܐ
ܐܘܪܚܗ ܢܛܘܪܬ ܡܢ ܟܠ ܒܥܠܕܒܒ̈ܐ ܒܝ̈ܫܐ ܘܡܪܝܪܐ
ܢܚܙܘܢܗ, ܘܢܫܬܟܚܘܢܗ, ܡܢ ܟܠ ܢܟܝ̈ܠܝܢ ܒܐܘܪܚܗ
ܢܬܒܪܘܢ ܒܝܬܗ ܕܦܠ: ܗ̈: ܗ: ܒܫܡܝܐ ܘܒܐܪܥܐ
ܒܠܘܬ ܡܪܢ, ܐܫܝܢܐ ܘܗܠܝܢܐ ܐܡܝܢ

§ 32 ܠܐܢܫ ܕܐܙܠ ܠܠܠܝܐ ܒܐܘܪܚܐ ܠܐ ܢܕܚܠ

ܒܫܡ ܐܒܐ ܘܒܪܐ ܘܪܘ: ܕܩܘܕܫܐ ܐܠܗܐ ܕܐܒܪܗܡ
ܘܕܝܣܚܩ ܘܕܝܥܩܘܒ ܐܠܗܐ ܕܐܒܗ̈ܬܢ ܒܢ̈ܝܐ ܘܙܪ̈ܥܐ
ܐܠܗܐ ܐܒܘܗ, ܕܡܪܢ ܝܫܘܥ ܡܫܝ: ܒܫܡܝܢ ܡܫܝܢ
ܘܡܫܬܒܚܝܢ ܠܥܠܡܝܢ ܒܫܡܐ ܕܝܗܒ ܦܠ: ܗ̈: ܗ:
ܒܐܘܪܚܐ ܕܠܗܘܢ, ܕܬܠܬܝܢ ܒܪ. ܢܦܩ ܐܢܬ ܠܦܓܪܗ
ܘܠܢܦܫܗ ܡܢ ܟܠ ܢܟܝ̈ܢܝܢ ܘܡܫܘܙܒ ܐܢܬ ܠܗ ܡܢ ܟܠ
ܫܘ̈ܟܠܝܢ ܐܚܪܢܐ ܕܗܘܝܬ ܒܗ ܝܘܣܦ ܒܐܪܒܐ ܕܡܨܪܝܢ
ܘܥܡ ܕܢܝܐܝܠ ܒܓܘܒܐ ܕܐܪ̈ܝܘܬܐ ܘܥܡ ܕܒܢ̈ܝ ܚܢܢܝܐ
ܒܐܬܘܢܐ ܕܢܘܪܐ ܠܐܪܡܝܐ ܒܓܘܒܐ ܕܛܝܢܐ ܘܐܦ
ܥܡ ܥܒܕܟ ܗܢܐ ܦܠ: ܗ̈: ܗ: ܘܡܛܠ ܐܢܬ ܡܪܝܗ
ܘܩܪܝܐ ܕܐܘܪܚܐ ܗܕܐ ܕܒܗ̇ ܚܝܘ ܘܢܣܒܐ ܫܘܡܠܝܐ
ܫܦܝܪܐ ܒܪ. ܡܫܦܫ ܐܢܬ ܠܗ ܫܘܒܩܢܐ ܘܦܘܪܩܢܐ
ܡܟܠܗ ܐܦ̈ܐ ܕܣܛܢܐ ܠܘܬ ܟܠܢܫ ܘܠܐܬܪܐ ܕܠܗ
ܐܙܠ ܐܗܦܟܝܗ, ܡܪܝ, ܒܪ. ܡܠܐ ܦܘܡܗ ܘܡܟܠܠܘܬܐ
ܘܠܒܝܗ ܬܫܒܘ: ܒܪ. ܒܚܕܘܬܐ ܘܒܪܘܪܐ ܢܗܦܘܟ ܠܒܝܬܗ
ܘܢܫܡ ܠܟ ܬܫܒܘ: ܘܐܘܕܝܐ ܘܬܘܕܝܬܐ ܘܫܘܒܚܬܐ
ܠܫܡܟ ܡܫܒܚܐ ܡܦܪܢܝܐ ܕܒܒ̈ܢܘܗܝ, ܘܡܫܬܒܚܐ
ܕܕܝܠܘܗܝ, ܐܡܝܢ

ܕܚܘ̈ܫܐ ܘܠܓܢ̈ܬܐ § 33

ܒܫܡ ܐܒܐ ܘܒܪܐ ܘܪܘܚܐ ܕܩܘ: ܒܫܡܟ ܐܠܗܐ
ܣܒܪܐ ܕܥܠܡܐ ܐܣܝ̈ܪܐ ܐܣܝܪܐ ܠܦܟܪܐ ܘܠܦܟܪܘܬ
ܠܟܠܒ ܐܝ̈ܕܝܐ ܕܐܢܫܐ ܘܠܢܩ̈ܘܫܐ ܬ̈ܠܝܐ ܘܡܫܪ̈ܝܐ
ܕܕܒܝܩܝܢ ܒܓܕܒܐ ܕܠܘܩܒܠ ܒܢ̈ܝܗ̇ ܕܟ̣ܠ: ܡ̈ܘ: ܗܠܝܢ
ܐܣܝܪܐ ܠܗܘܢ ܡܢ ܪܝܫܗ ܘܡܢ ܒܢ̈ܘܗܝ ܘܡܢ ܦܘ̈ܡܗܝ
ܘܡܢ ܟܘܠܝܐ ܕܪܝܫܗ ܘܠܐ ܢܫܠܛܘܢ ܠܢܩܘܫܐ
ܠܟܠܗܘܢ ܒܪ̈ܝܗ ܘܠܐ ܒܦܚ ܡܢ ܗܕ̈ܡܘܗܝ ܕܟ̣ܠ: ܡ̈ܘ:
ܒܨܠܘܬ ܡܪܬ̇ ܡܪܝܡ ܒܬܘܠܬܐ ܘܕܡܪܝ ܝܘܚܢܢ
ܡܥܡܕܢܐ ܘܕܡܪܝ ܐܒܪܗܡ ܪܒܐ ܘܕܡܪܝ ܐܒܪܗܡ
ܩܕܘܢܝܐ ܘܕܡܪܝ ܫܡܥܘܢ ܒܪܨܒܥܐ ܐܡܝܢ

ܕܣܘܬܪܢܐ ܕܒܝܬܐ § 34

ܒܫܡ ܐܒܐ ܘܒܪܐ ܘܪ: ܕܩܘ: ܗ̇ܘ ܕܫܒܩ ܐܠܦܐ
ܒܡܕܒܪܐ ܘܐܟܠܘ ܡܢ ܠܚܡܐ ܙܥܘܪܐ ܘܗܘܘ ܣܒܥܝܢ
ܗܝ ܦܬܘܪܐ ܕܢܘܗܪܐ ܡܠܝܐ ܘܡܬܪܝܐ ܕܢܐܟܠܘܢ
ܡܣ̈ܟܢܐ ܢܣܒܥܘܢ ܘܢܬܒܪܟܐ ܒܝܬܗ ܢܬܬܪܣܐ ܟܠ
ܬܟܒܝܪ ܟܠܗܘܢ ܢܬܒܪܟܘܢ ܐܝܟ ܦܬܘܪ ܐܒܪܗܡ
ܚܒܝܒܐ. ܕܗܘܐ ܡܠܟܐ ܘܟܗܢܐ ܘܫܠܝܡܘܢ ܒܡ
ܢܘܣܐ ܘܕܝܐܢܐܠ ܒܡ ܡܫܝܚܐ ܡܘܦܠܝܣܘܣ ܘܕܒܝܐ
ܗܒܠܐ ܡܪܝ ܢܬܒܪܟܢ ܒܝܬܐ ܗܢܐ ܒܝܬ ܕܒܟܒܝܟ
ܒܠܦ̈ܬܐ ܘܢܬܪܬܚܢ ܒܪܟ ܡܪܝ ܠܡܦܠܚܢܘܗܝ ܒܪܒܪܟܢ
ܦܠܚ̈ܘܗܝ ܒܪܟܪܝ ܒܝܬܗ ܒܪܟܪܝ ܟܡܘܪ̈ܘܗܝ ܐܝܟ
ܡܪܢ ܟܠ ܒܝܬܗ ܘܐܫܪܐ ܒܠܒܗ ܒܡܘܪ̈ܒܬܐ ܕܟܪܝܢ
ܟܐܡ̈ܐ ܘܐܟܡܗ̈ܬܐ ܗܟܢ ܚܝܠܐ ܘܐܬܘ̈ܬܐ ܦܬܘܪܗ
ܢܒܪܝܢ ܘܟܡܘܪܗ ܢܬܪܬܚ ܒܒܢ̈ܘܗܝ ܢܬܚܣܡܘܢ
ܣܘܒ̈ܥܘܢ ܘܡܫܬܥܘܢ ܢܬܚܡܘܢ ܗܢܐ ܘܟܒܠܝܡ
ܘܠܥܠܡ ܥܠܡܝܢ ܐܡܝܢ

§ 35 ܐܣܘܪܐ ܕܦܘܡܐ ܕܕܐܒ̈ܐ ܡܢ ܒܥܝ̈ܪܐ ܘܡܢ ܚܝ̈ܘܬܐ

ܒܫܡ ܐܒܐ ܘܒܪܐ ܘܪܘܚܐ ܕܩܘܕ: ܒܚܝܠܘܬܗ ܘܒܟܒܘܬܗ
ܘܬܫܒܘܚܬܗ ܘܬܚܢܢܘܬܗ ܕܡܪܝ، ܕܐܚܝܕ ܟܠ ܢܦܫܐ ܕܚܝܬ
ܠܓܘܒܐ ܕܐܪ̈ܥܬܐ ܒܕܘܒ̈ܐ ܠܐ ܢܚܒܠܘܢ، ܐܣܝܪܝܢ
ܘܚܬܝܡܝܢ ܘܟܠܝܠܝܢ ܦܘܡܝ̈ܗܘܢ ܕܕܐܒ̈ܐ ܘܕܒ̈ܐ
ܘܐܪ̈ܝܘܬܐ ܦܘܡ ܟܠܗ ܚܝܘܬܐ ܡܚܒܠܢܝܬܐ ܡܢ
ܒܠܚܘܕ ܕܐܝܬ ܠܗ ܘܕܗܘܐ ܠܗ ܠܝ: ܬܘ: ܗ: ܒܫܘܦܪܗ
ܕܡܫܬܐ ܢܒܝܐ ܘܒܒܪܘܬܗ ܕܒܠܝܡܘܢ ܒܪ ܢܘܚ ܡܢ
ܚܝ̈ܘܬܗ، ܘܡܢ ܒܥܝ̈ܪܗ، ܕܦ: ܒ: ܬܘܒ ܐܣܝܪܝܢ
ܘܚܬܝܡܝܢ ܘܟܠܝܠܝܢ ܦܘܡܝ̈ܗܘܢ ܘܠܫܢ̈ܝܗܘܢ ܕܐ̈ܝܠܝܢ
ܕܗܘܐ ܦܬܝܚܐ ܠܐ ܢܟܐܦ ܘܐܢ ܢܒܥܐ ܠܐ ܢܦܬܚ
ܒܚܝ̈ܠܘܬܗ ܕܙܟܝ ܗܘܪܡܝܙܕ ܘܒܟܒܘܫܬܗ ܕܡܪܝ، ܐܠܗܐ
ܘܒܚܢܢܘܬܗ ܕܡܪܝ، ܕܐܚܝܕ ܢܦܫ̈ܬܐ ܢܬܐܣܪ ܦܘܡܐ
ܕܕܐܒ̈ܐ ܘܕܒ̈ܐ ܘܟܠܗ ܚܝܘܬܐ ܐܡܝܢ **ܒܪܝ ܟܠ**
ܡܚܝܠܐ

§ 36 ܐܣܘܪܐ ܕܫ̈ܠܗܒܐ ܕܕ̈ܓܠܐ

ܒܫܡ ܐܒܐ ܘܒܪܐ ܘܪܘ: ܕܩܘ: ܘܒܫܡ ܐܗܝܗ
ܐܫܪܗܝܗ ܐܠܫܕܝ، ܐܕܘܢܝ ܡܪܝܐ ܨܒܐܘܬ ܘܒܫܡ
ܒܪܣܦܪܘܣ ܘܒܫܡ ܙܟܝ ܗܘܪܡܝܙܕ ܘܕܡܪܝ، ܦܬܘܩ
ܐܣܝܪܐ ܘܡܚܬܡܐ ܘܦܩܝܕܐ ܘܓܙܝܪܐ ܠܗܘܢ ܠܫ̈ܠܗܒܐ
ܒܢ̈ܫܐ ܘܟܠܗ ܦܓܥܐ ܕܕ̈ܝܘܐ ܒܠܠܝܐ ܘܒܐܝܡܡܐ
ܗܘܝܐ ܡܢ ܕ̈ܝܘܐ ܒܢ̈ܫܐ ܘܡܢ ܫܠ̈ܗܒܐ ܕ̈ܓܠܐ ܡܢ
ܫܪ̈ܘܗܝ، ܕܦ: ܬܘ: ܗܠܝܢ ܐܝܟ ܕܦܓܪܬ ܠܠܝܠܝܐ ܡܢ
ܗܘ ܕܟܒܫܬ ܡܒܘܪܐ ܒܡܪܝ ܗܘܐ ܗܒܝܐ ܢܬܪܣܘܢ

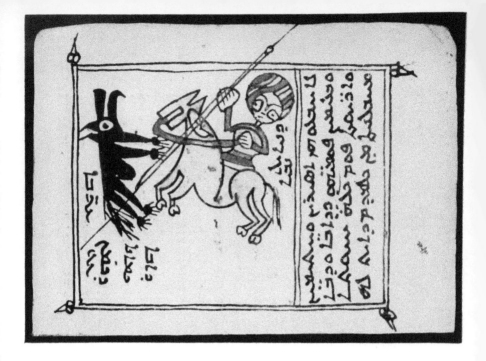

Cod. A, p. 47

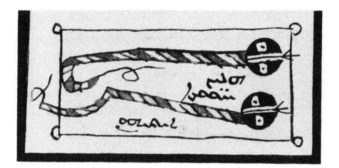

Cod. A, p. 49

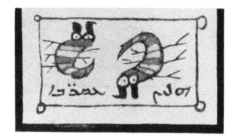

Cod. A, p. 50

To face p. 22

ܘܠܐ ܡܝܪܐ (sic)ܘܒܠܐܬ ܘܣܡܪ (sic)ܘܒܠܟܐܬܐ ܘܠܝܐ
---

1 I read ܠܕ for ܡܢ.   2 Probably ܘܩܣܐ.
3 Add ܘܐܪ ܬܪܡܣܒ.   4 Shortened for ܪܕܒܝܠܩܐ.

§ 39 ܘܚܙܝܐ ܕܠܐ ܡܓܠܝܐ ܠܗ ܒܢܝܐ ܒܫܢܬܐ

ܒܫܡ ܐܒܐ ܘܒܪܐ ܘܪܘܚܐ ܕܩܘ: ܠܫܒܒܐ ܐܡܝܢ
ܠܬ̈ܓܠܐ ܒܢ̈ܘܗܝ, ܕܓܒܪܐ ܒܢܝܐ ܘܫܪܒܬܐ ܠܐܢܫܐ
ܫܦܝܬܘܢ ܥܠ ܒܘ̈ܪܟܝܗܘܢ ܘܐܙܠܝܬܘܢ ܥܠ ܪ̈ܓܠܝܗܘܢ[1]
ܘܡܗܠܟܝܬܘܢ ܥܠ ܐܝ̈ܕܝܗܘܢ ܐܡܪܝܢ ܒܢ̈ܝܐ ܒܢ̈ܘܗܝ,
ܕܓܒܪܐ ܒܢܝܐ ܘܫܪܒܬܐ ܫܦܝܢ ܥܠ ܒܘ̈ܪܟܝܢ ܘܐܙܠܝܢ
ܥܠ ܐܝ̈ܕܝܢ ܘܡܗܠܟܝܢ ܥܠ ܪ̈ܓܠܝܢ ܕܢܐܟܘܠ ܒܣܪܐ
ܘܢܫܬܐ[2] ܒܫ̈ܘܦܝܢ ܘܟܕ ܣܒܬ ܐܢܘܢ ܐܣܝܪܬ ܐܢܘܢ
ܒܫܡ ܐܒܐ ܘܒܪܐ ܘܪܘ: ܕܩܘ: ܡܬܘܡܝܐ ܘܬܠܝܬܝܐ
ܕܐܠܗܐ ܡܫܪܝܬܘܢ ܘܐܣܝܪܝܬܘܢ ܒܫܡ ܓܒܪܝܠ
ܘܡܝܟܐܝܠ ܘܥܙܪܐܝܠ ܬܠܬܐ ܡܠܐܟ̈ܐ ܩܕ̈ܝܫܐ
ܒܫܡ ܗ̇ܘ ܡܠܐܟܐ ܕܐܕ̈ܢ ܐܝܬܬܐ[3] ܕܗܪܘܬ[4] ܪܫܗ̇
ܒܡܒܠܠ ܣܓܕܒܒܐ ܡܕܝܢܐ ܘܒ ܫܡ ܡܪܗܘܢ
ܕܡܠܐܟ̈ܐ ܕܠܐ ܬܐܙܠܘܢ ܒܐܘܪܚܗܘܢ ܘܠܐ ܬܫܠܛܘܢ
ܡܐܙܠܬܗܘܢ ܘܫܒ̈ܝܠܗܘܢ ܠܒܢܘܪ ܡܪܝܐ ܘܢܦܫܗ ܘܦܓܪܗ
ܕܪ̈ܚܡܘܗܝ ܘܒܢ̈ܬܐ. ܕܒܢ̈ܝܗܘܢ ܡܢ ܡܢܝܢ ܕܠ: ܬܗ: ܘܠ: ܗ:
ܐܝܟ ܕܡܬܦܠܛ ܬܢܝܢܐ ܡܢ ܩܕܡ ܚܠܒܠܐ ܢܬܦܠܛܘܢ
ܒܫܡ ܐܒܐ ܘܒܪܐ ܘܪܘ: ܕܩܘ: ܒܫܡ ܐܒܐ ܐܒܗܘܬܐ
ܒܫܡ ܒܪܐ ܒܪܘܬܐ ܒܫܡ ܪܘ: ܕܩܘ: ܢܦܩܘܬܐ
ܒܫܡܐ ܕܬܠܝܬܝܘܬܐ ܡܫܒܚܬܐ ܗܫܐ ܘܒܟܠܙܒܢ
ܘܠܥܠܡ ܥܠܡܝܢ ܐܡܝܢ

[1] MS. ܪ̈ܓܠܗܘܢ.

[2] Add ܠܕܡܐ according to B, 102.

[3] MS. ܐܝܬܬܗ.

[4] MS. ܕܗܪܘܬܗ.

§ 40 ܕܪܚܡܢܘܬܐ ܕܠܘܬ ܟܠ ܐܢܫ

ܒܫܡ ܐܒܐ ܘܒܪܐ ܘܪܘ: ܕܩܘ: ܐܝܟܢܐ ܕܪܚܡ
ܐܠܗܐ ܠܟܠܗܘܢ ܘܡܒܥܐ ܠܐ̈ܢܫܐ ܡܬ̈ܘܒܐ ܒܛܝܒܘܬܗ
ܘܐܝܟܢܐ ܕܪܚܡ ܐܠܗܐ ܠܒܪܢܫܐ ܘܦܠܓ ܡܕܡܘܗܝ
ܡܟܐ ܕܝܘܣܦ ܘܐܝܟܢܐ ܕܪܚܡ ܐܠܗܐ ܠܝܘܣܦ ܘܫܠܛ
ܥܒܕܐ ܥܒܕܗ ܡܪܐ ܥܠ ܟܠܗ ܡܨܪܝܢ ܗܘܝܐ ܡܪܐ
ܐܠܗܐ ܫܠܝܛܐ ܐܘܪܚܐ ܢܘܪܐ ܕܪܚܡܬܗ ܕܝܠܟ: ܗ̈ܘ:
ܗ: ܟܠܗ ܠܒܐ ܕܫܠܝܛܢܐ ܕܫܢܐ ܘܐܡܝ̈ܢܐ ܘܪ̈ܒܢܐ
ܘܦܩ̈ܕܐ ܘܦܩܘ̈ܕܐ ܐܣܝܪܢܐ ܘܒܠܒܢܐ ܦܘܩ̈ܕܢܘܗܝ
ܘܠܥܒ̈ܕܘܗܝ ܒܗܘ ܫܠܝܐ ܕܐܠܝܐ ܢܒܝܐ ܕܐܣܪ ܠܫܡܝܐ
ܬܠܬ ܫܢ̈ܝܢ ܘܫܬܐ ܝ̈ܪܚܝܢ ܘܠܐ ܢܚܬ ܡܛܪܐ ܥܠ
ܐܪܥܐ ܘܒܫܡ ܐܡܪܗ ܐܫܬܪܝܢܐ ܐܠܝܫܥ ܐܕܘܢ
ܡܪܝܐ ܠܥܠܡܝܢ ܐܡܝܢ

§ 41 ܥܡܫ̈ܝܐ ܕܒܝܬܗ ܕܡܠܟܐ ܥܠܝܡܘܗܝ ܕܫܥܢܝܢ ܠܡܕܡ ܡ̈ܠܟܐ

ܒܫܡ ܐܒܐ ܘܒܪܐ ܘܪܘ: ܕܩܘܕܫܐ ܗܘܦܟܝ ܦܬܓܡ
ܠܟܦܝ ܕܫܢܬ ܦܝܕܟܝܬ ܥܫܠܝܬ ܪܡܕܝܬ ܘܫܠܝܟܬ
ܠܟܝܬܟܝ ܥܠܠܬ ܬܘܪܝܦ ܡܦܥܕܬ ܕܩܦܝܬ
ܟܪܝܟܬ ܦܝܢܬ ܢܣܒܬ ܥܠܠܬ ܒܬܟܬ ܦܝܢܬ

---

[1] Words encircling illustration. For this whole section *see* Translation and Appendix.

[2] MS. ܢܘܚܝܫ.   [3] MS. ܪܒܠܝܢܘܚ.   [4] MS. ܒܪܪܡ.

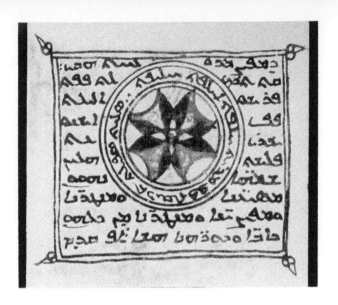

Cod. A, p. 54

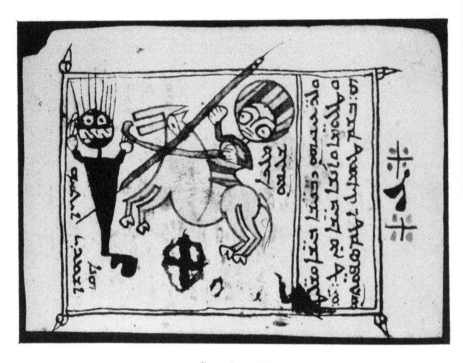

Cod. A, p. 55

To face p. 26

ܒܝܘܡܐ ܕܐܪܒܥܐ ܐܪܒܥܝܢ ܥܢ̈ܝܢ ܡܬܚܫܒܝܢ ܗܘܘ
ܠܐܠܗܐ ܡܛܠ ܕܢܘܗܪܐ ܡܒܕܪܢܐ ܕܚܠܒܐ ܗܢܐ
ܢܘܗܪܐ ܒܪܒܐ ܒܟܠܗ ܐܝܟ ܚܠܐ ܕܡܫܬ̈ܚܐ ܒܗܘ̇
ܡܠܐܟܐ ܕܝܢ[1] ܟܘ̈ܠܐ ܒܚܙܘܪܐ ܕܐܬܚܙ̈ܝܬܗܘܢ
ܗܒܠܐ ܢܘܪܐ ܘܢܬܬܠܝܛ ܫܠܒܐ ܗܢܐ ܕܦ: ܒ: ܕܦ:
ܘܐܝܟ ܠܚܝܫܘ ܢܗܘܬܐ ܡܫܡܫܗ ܘܡܢܗܪܢܗ ܘܐܝܟ
ܡܒܘܒܐ ܕܙܢܝܐ ܒܪܝ̈ ܒܫܡܝܐ ܫܦܝܪܐ ܘܡܫܒܚܐ
ܕܐܠܗܐ ܚܝܐ ܐܝܟ ܘܐܡܝܢ **ܒܪܝܟ** ܒܠ ܠܐ ܡܠܝܐ
ܘܐܘܒܠ ܡܛܠ ܬܘܪܬܐ ܘܡܒܝܢܗ ܒܢܘ:[2] ܘܡܒܝܢܬ̇
ܒܫܠܡܐ

§ 45 **ܐܘܪܚܐ ܕܫܪܝܬܐ** ܒܪܝܟ ܥܠ ܒܥܬܐ **ܘܐܘܠܨܢܗܝ**

ܒܫܡ ܐܒܐ ܘܒܪܐ ܘܪܘ: ܕܩܘ: ܐܘܪܚܐ ܠܗ̇ ܠܫܪܝܬܗ
ܕܦ: ܒ: ܕܦ: ܐܝܟ ܬܘܪܐ ܒܒܝܪܐ ܘܐܝܟ ܦܘܦܝܢܐ
ܒܦܓܕܬܐ ܘܐܝܟ ܡܝܢܬܐ ܒܡܒܪܐ ܘܐܝܟ ܦܪܝܬܐ
ܒܦܝܐ ܘܒܢܝܒܐ ܐܘܪܚܐ ܠܗ̇ ܠܫܪܝܬܗ ܒܗܘ̇ ܚܝܠܐ
ܕܐܘܪ ܐܠܗܐ ܢܒܝܐ ܫܡܥܝܐ ܬܠܬ ܫܢܝܢ ܘܫܬܐ ܝܪ̈ܚܝܢ
ܘܠܐ ܢܚܬ ܡܛܪܐ ܥܠ ܐܪܥܐ ܒܗ ܒܗܘ̇ ܚܝܠܐ
ܬܐܬܐ ܘܬܬܐܣܪ ܫܪܝܬܗ ܕܦ: ܒ: ܕܦ: ܒܗܘ̇ ܚܝܠܐ
ܕܐܣܪ ܡܪܢ ܘܡܦܪܢܘܣ ܠܢܒ̈ܝܐ ܒܟܝ̈ܠܬܐ ܕܠܐ ܠܐ ܢܬܠ̈ܟ
ܘܠܡܫܪܬܐ ܕܠܐ ܢܫܟܠܘܢ ܐܘܪܚܐ ܠܗ̇ ܠܫܪܝܬܗ ܕܦ:
ܩܘ̈: ܗ: ܐܡܝܢ ܘܐܡܝܢ

[1] MS. ܕܝܐܕ. [2] Shortened for ܒܢܘܪܐ.

§ 46 ܚܪܡܐ ܕܡܪܝ ܫܠܝܛܐ ܕܚܒܫ ܠܪܘܚܐ ܒܝܫܬܐ

ܒܫܡ ܐܒܐ ܘܒܪܐ ܘܪܘ: ܕܩܘ: ܨܠܘܬܗ ܘܒܥܘܬܗ ܘܬܟܫܦܬܗ ܘܬܫܡܫܬܗ ܕܡܪܝ ܫܠܝܛܐ ܕܨܠܝ ܘܒܥܐ ܡܢ ܐܠܗܐ ܒܒܥܘܬܐ ܕܒܡܠܠܐ ܘܐܡܪ ܡܪܝ ܝܫܘܥ ܡܫܝܚܐ ܒܠܚܡ ܕܢܬܒܪ ܫܡܟ ܡܪܝܐ ܘܫܡܗ ܕܠܗ ܒܒܪܝܟ ܫܠܝܛܐ ܠܐ ܬܬܩܪܒ ܠܗ ܪܘܚܐ ܣܘܡܡܬܐ ܘܠܐ ܙܪ: ܒܝܫܬܐ ܡܢ ܦܓܪܗ ܘܡܢ ܢܦܫܗ[1] ܕܦ: ܒ: ܕܦ: ܒܨܠܘܬ ܡܪܝ ܐܘܓܝܢ ܛܘܒܢܐ ܐܡܝܢ

§ 47 ܐܣܘܪܐ ܕܦܘܡܐ ܕܨܦܪܐ ܘܕܒܥܘܒܪܐ

ܒܫܡ ܐܒܐ ܘܒܪܐ ܘܪܘܚܐ ܕܩܘ: ܐܣܘܪܐ ܦܘܡܐ ܕܐܘܟܠܐ ܘܕܒܥܘܒܪܐ ܘܕܨܦܪܐ ܘܕܦܪܚܬܐ ܘܒܒܢܝܪܐ ܐܣܘܪܐ ܠܗܘܢ ܒܒܢܝܐ ܚܝܐ ܕܨܠܒܐ ܡܪܢܝܐ ܘܒܨܠܘܬܗ ܕܡܪܬܝ ܡܪܝܡ ܛܘܒܢܝܬܐ ܘܒܫܡܗ ܕܗܢܐ ܕܐܣܪ ܠܫܡܝܐ ܠܐܪܥܐ ܘܠܡܩܒܘܥܐ ܘܢ̈ܗܪܐ ܘܒܚܝܪܐ ܘܦܪܚܬܐ ܕܫܡܝܐ ܘܬܘܠܥܐ ܐܣܘܪܐ ܦܘܡܐ ܕܚܝ̈ܘܬܐ ܘܕܐܘܟܠܐ ܘܕܒܥܘܒܪܐ ܘܕܨܦܪܐ ܘܕܦܪܚܬܐ ܡܢ ܚܩ̈ܠܬܗ ܕܦ: ܦ̈: ܗ: ܐܣܘܪܐ ܠܗܘܢ ܒܫܡܗ̇ ܕܒܢܬ ܡܢ ܫܡܫܐ ܢܦܩ ܐܪ̈ܚܐ ܡܒܢ̈ܝܐ ܐܣܘܪܐ ܠܦܘܡܐ ܕܐܘܟܠܐ ܘܕܒܥܘܒܪܐ[2] ܘܕܨܦܪܐ ܘܕܦܪܚܬܐ ܘܒܒܢܝܪܐ ܐܣܘܪܐ ܠܗܘܢ ܒܒܢܝܐ ܚܝܐ ܕܨܠܒܐ ܡܪܢܝܐ ܒܨܠܘܬ ܡܪܬܝ ܡܪܝܡ ܛܘܒܢܝܬܐ ܡܢ ܫܠܡܗ ܕܦ: ܒ: ܕܦ: ܐܡܝܢ

[1] This may be an error for ܠܦܓܪܗ ܘܠܢܦܫܗ (*cf.* Translation).

[2] ܒ omitted in MS.

§ 48 ܐܣܘܪܐ ܕܢܘܪܐ ܡܢ ܓ̈ܠܐ ܘܡܢ ܓܕܝ̈ܫܐ

ܒܫܡ ܚܝܠܐ ܐܠܗܝܐ ܕܕܥܟ ܐܬܘܢܐ ܕܢܘܪܐ ܡܢ
ܕܒܝܬ ܚܢܢܝܐ ܘܥܙܪܝܐ ܘܡܝܫܐܝܠ ܗܘ ܢܕܥܟ ܢܘܪܐ
ܘܫܠܗܒܝܬܐ ܕܠܐ ܬܬܚܒܠ ܒܓܕܝ̈ܫܘܗܝ ܕܚܛ̈ܐ
ܘܕ̈ܓܠܗ ܘܠܐ ܒܒܝܬܗ ܕܦ: ܒ: ܕܦ: ܒܫܡ ܚܝܠܐ
ܕܕܥܟ ܐܬܘܢܐ ܕܒܒܠ، ܠܢܘܪܓܝܣ ܗܘ ܢܕܥܟ ܢܘܪܐ
ܘܫܠܗܒܝܬܐ ܘܠܐ ܬܬܚܒܠ ܘܠܐ ܬܬܢܣܪ ܠܐ
ܒܓܕܝ̈ܫܘܗܝ ܕܚܛ̈ܐ ܘܠܐ ܕܓܠ̈ܘܗܝ، ܠܐ ܒܒܝܬܗ ܕܦ:
ܗ̇: ܗ: ܬܘܒ ܐܣܘܪܐ ܘܦܘܪܕܢܐ ܘܡܒܕܒܕܢܐ ܠܦܪܙܠܐ
ܘܬܘܒ ܐܣܘܪܐ ܠܟܐܦܐ ܕܠܐ ܢܦܩ ܡܢܗܘܢ ܢܘܪܐ
ܐܣܘܪܐ ܠܢܘܪܐ ܕܠܐ ܬܘܩܕ ܙ̈ܘܥܐ ܘܡܠ̈ܬܠܐ ܒܒܪ̈ܐ
ܕܡܠܬܗ ܘܡܙ̈ܠܓܐ ܬܗܘܐ ܡܙܪ ܡܟܒ ܙ̈ܘܥܐ ܡܙܪ̈ܩܝܢ
ܡܛ̈ܠܐ ܐܣܘܪܐ ܐܢܕܪ̈ܝܫܘܢ ܘܙ̈ܠܝܡܘܢ ܚܝܡܘܢ ܒܚܠܝܡ
ܢܗܘܐ ܕܒܟܐ ܐܣܘܪܐ ܠܦܪܙܠܐ ܘܠܟܐܦܐ ܕܠܐ ܬܦܘܩ
ܡܢܗܘܢ ܢܘܪܐ ܒܫܡ ܡܠܬܐ ܕܐܠܗܐ ܡܠܠ ܕܐܣܪ
ܠܫܡܝܐ ܬܠܬ ܫܢ̈ܝܢ ܘܫܬܐ ܝܪ̈ܚܝܢ ܠܐ ܢܚܬ ܡܛܪܐ
ܥܠ ܐܪܥܐ ܗܘ ܒܫܡ ܡܠܬܐ ܐܣܘܪܐ ܠܦܪܙܠܐ
ܘܠܟܐܦܐ ܕܠܐ ܬܦܘܩ ܡܢܗܘܢ ܢܘܪܐ ܕܠܐ ܬܕܠܩ
ܘܠܐ[1] ܬܘܩܕ ܠܟܠܗ ܘܠܐ ܠܒܝ̈ܬܘܗܝ، ܕܦ: ܕܦ: ܒ:
ܐܡܝܢ

§ 49 ܕܕܒܒܐ ܕܐܘܪ̈ܬܐ ܒܚܫܝܪܐ

ܘܕܪܝܐ ܐܬܒܛܠ ܘܡܒܒܒܐ ܕܡ̈ܫܚܐ ܐܣܬܒܪܘ
ܗܒܠܐ ܠܫܬܒܪ ܕܡܣܗ ܕܦ: ܒ: ܕܦ: ܐܡܝܢ
ܒܬܘܒ ܡܢ ܕܡܣܗ ܒܫܘܢܐ ܕܫ̈ܦܠܐ ܒܝܬ ܒܢܘ̈ܗܝ،

[1] Words ܬܕܠܩ ܘܠܐ repeated in MS. by mistake.

§ 50 ܕܬܘ̈ܠܥܐ ܕܠܐ ܒܓܦܢ

ܒܫܡ ܐܒܐ ܘܒܪܐ ܘܪܘ: ܕܩܘ: ܒܫܡ ܡܠܐܟܐ
ܘܡܫܡܫܢܘܗܝ ܘܡܪܓܠܠܘܗܝ ܘܣܦܪ̈ܣܝܢ ܘܫܘܫܝܢܘܗܝ ܗܠܝܢ
ܫܒܥܐ ܐܣ̈ܪܝ ܕܕܡܟܘ ܫܒܥܬܐ ܬܠܬܡܐܐ ܘܫܒܥܝܢ
ܫܒܥܝܢ ܫܢ̈ܝܢ ܗܟܢܐ ܢܫܠܐ ܘܢܕܚܩܝܘܗܝ ܦ: ܒ: ܕܦ:
ܘܢܕܚܩܝܘܗܝ ܥܒܕܬܐ ܕܓܦܢܐ ܚܠܠܬܐ ܒܟܠܗ ܬܘܠܥ ܢܒܢ̈ܝܐ
ܘܫܠܝܢܐ ܐܡܝܢ ܘܐܡܝܢ

§ 51 ܐܣܝ ܕܒܒܢܝܢ ܒܗ ܚ̈ܙܝܐ

ܚܙܘ ܘܡܬܒܪܘܗܝ ܒܒܢܝܢ ܗܘܘ ܚ̈ܙܝܐ ܘܠܐ ܡܫܟܚܝܢ
ܗܘܘ ܕܢܫܒܩܘܢ ܗܘܘ ܠܗܘܢ ܡܘܬܐ ܒܢܝܐ ܐܘܪܚܐ ܗܒܢܐ
ܢܬܚܠܠܘܢ ܚ̈ܙܝܐ ܘܐܣܘܪ̈ܐ ܕܚܙܝܘܬܐ ܒܝܬ ܦ: ܒ:
ܕܦ: ܐܡܝܢ ܘܐܡܝܢ ܘܐܡܝܢ

§ 52 ܚܪܡܐ ܕܐܡ̈ܗܬܐ ܐܘܒܕܢܬ
ܕܦܪ̈ܕܝܣܐ ܕܢܫܘ ܠܟܠ ܒܐ̈ܬܝܢ

ܒܫܡ ܐܒܐ ܘܒܪܐ ܘܪܘ: ܕܩܘ: ܒܝܠܘܬ ܕܐܡ̈ܗܬܐ
ܒܐ̈ܬܐ ܘܙܕ̈ܝܩܐ ܦܘܠܘܣ ܘܐܢܕܪܝܣ ܘܡܬܝܘܣ ܘܐܦܪܝܡ ܘܐܘܪܣܝܣ
ܘܣܦܪ̈ܣܝܢ ܘܡܪܝ، ܦܘܠܐ ܫܡܥܘܢܐ ܚܢܢܝܐ ܘܐܠܝܐ
ܦܘ̈ܠܝܐ ܡܪܝ، ܘܡܪܝ ܡܒܪܟܐ ܡܪܝ، ܘܡܪܝ ܦܠܝܐ
ܡܪܝ، ܘܡܪܝ ܒܥܒܪܐ ܡܪܝ، ܘܡܪܝ ܐܟܣܦܢܐ ܡܪܝ،
ܘܡܪܝ ܡܘܠܝܐ ܡܪܝ، ܘܡܪܝ ܢܘܠܐ ܡܪܝ، ܘܡܪܝ ܙܟܝܐ
ܡܪܝ، ܘܡܪܝ ܕܡܒܕܪܐ ܡܪܝ، ܘܡܪܝ[1] ܕܗܒܐ ܡܪܝ، ܘܡܪܝ
ܦܘܡܝܢܐ ܡܪܝ، ܘܡܪܝ ܒܪܐܒܓܝ ܡܪܝ، ܘܡܪܝ ܒܪܡܪܬܐ
ܡܪܝ، ܘܡܪܝ ܒܪܒܕܬܐ ܡܪܝ، ܘܡܪܝ ܝܘܚܢܢ ܡܪܝ، ܘܡܪܝ

[1] Supply ܦܘܡܐ.

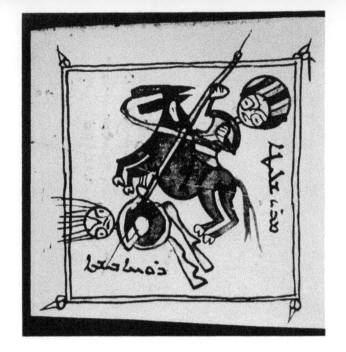

COD. A, P. 58

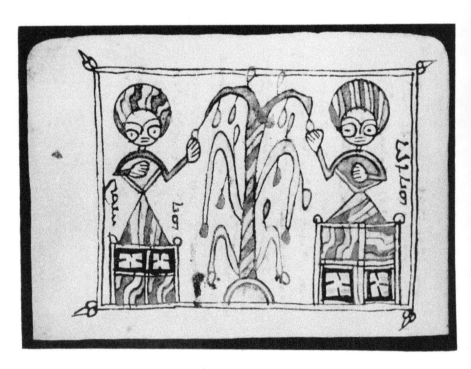

COD. A, P. 64

To face p. 30

---

1 MS. *sic*; same in Cod. B.M.   2 MS. *sic*; read ܐܝܠܟ.

3 MS. ܪܢܝ *cf.* Cod. B, 48.   4 MS. ܚܠܢܡ.

5 Read either ܕܕܚܘܪܢ or ܕܪܢܚܢ.   6 Omitted in MS.

ܒܡܪܝܐ ܘܒܢܝܢܐ ܗܕܝܢܐ ܕܒܢܝܢܗ̇ ܐܬܪܐ ܕ̇ܦ: ܒ: ܕ̇ܦ:
ܡܛܠ ܗܢܐ ܐܠܗܐ ܢܒܪܟ ܘܢܫܒܚ[1] ܠܥܠܡ ܡܢ
ܡܫܒܚ ܘܡܒܪܟ ܡܢ ܐܪܒܥܐ ܕܗܘ̈ܝܐ ܕ̇ܦ: ܒ: ܕ̇ܦ:
ܒܫܡ ܐܗܝܐ ܐܫܪܗܝܐ ܐܠܫܕܝ ܐܕܘܢܝ ܡܪܝܐ ܨܒܐܘܬ
ܐܢܐ ܦܩܘܢܐ ܠܗ̇ ܒܐܪܒܥܐ ܐܠܗܐ ܡܐܣܝܐ ܠܗ̇
ܒܫܡܗܐ ܐܡ ܘܐܡܝܢ **ܫܘܬܟܐ** ܒܫܡܝܢ ܡܪܘܬܢ
ܡܪܝ ܐܒܘܢ ܕܒܫܡܝܐ ܒܪܘܡܪܝ ܠܟ: ܩ̈: ܗ: ܘܠܟ
ܡܪܝ ܠܟ: ܩ̈: ܗ: ܘܫܒܚ ܠܟ: ܩ̈: ܗ: ܘܫܘܬܪ ܡܪܝ
ܠܟ: ܩ̈: ܗ: ܘܒܪܟ ܡܪܝ ܠܟ: ܩ̈: ܗ: ܕܫܡܝܢ
ܘܫܢܝܐ ܕܐܠܗܘܬܟ ܢܬܦܢܘܢ ܐܣܝܢܐܝܬ ܚܠ ܟ:
ܩ̈: ܗ: ܗܫܐ ܘܒܟܠܙܒܢ ܘܠܥܠܡ ܥܠܡܝܢ ܐܡܝܢ

§ 54 **ܒܫܡ ܡܪܢ ܟܬܒܢܐ ܚܘܫܒܢ**
ܒܪ̈ܝܬܐ ܡܢ ܡܢܘ ܚܪܫ ܠܗ
ܚܘܫܒ ܫܡܗ ܘܫܡܗ ܕܐܡܗ
ܘܐܦܩ ܐܢܘܢ ܟ: ܟ:
ܐܢ ܚܕ ܦܐܫ ܠܟ

ܒܫܡ ܚܕܒܫܒܐ ܗܘܐ ܒܦܘܪܗܢܐ ܒܡܕܢܚ ܫܡܫܐ
ܚܢܢܐ ܒܫܢܬܐ ܐܫܬܝܗ̇ ܡܢ ܪܫܗ ܘܡܢ ܟܬܦܗ ܘܡܢ
ܪܓܠܘܗܝ: ܟ: ܘܡܫ̈ܟܢ ܦܐܫ **ܒܡܨܪܐ ܡܪܝ**
ܘܫܠܡ ܒܬܒܬܐ ܕܒܢܝܐ ܒܢܫܬܐ **ܐܢ ܬܪܝܢ**
ܦܐܫ ܠܟ ܒܫܡ ܬܪܝܢ ܒܫܒܐ ܐܬܘܗܝ، ܒܣܘܪܐ
ܫܢܬܐ ܐܬܘܗܝ، ܡܪܒܥܐ ܡܢ ܒܪܫܗ ܘܡܢ ܚܝܟܗ ܘܡܢ

[1] Read ܘܢܫܬܒܚܘܢ.

---

[1] Only the tops of the last two letters are visible.

[2] Most probably so.

[3] The ܒ in the MS. is erased.

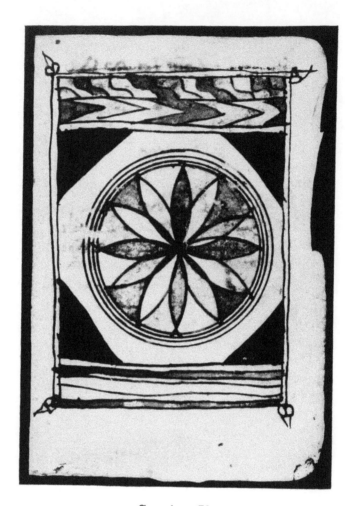

Cod. A, p. 73

To face p. 34

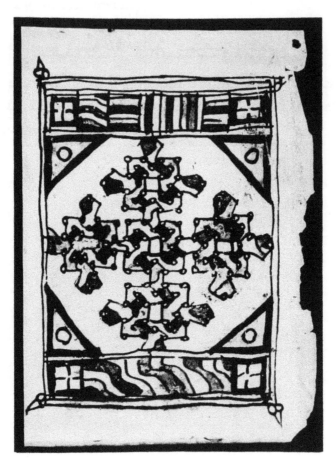

COD. A, P. 74

1 ܟܠ ܚܝܠܗ ܕܡܪܢ ܢܥܒܕ ܡܥܢܝܐ
ܡܥܢܝܢ ܠܡܫܒܚܬ [ܢܘ]ܗܪܐ
ܕܒܢ̈ܝܢܫܐ

§ 1 2 ܡܢ ܟܠ ܡܕܡ
ܘܕܡܝܬ ܠܝܠܘܬܐ
ܗ̇ܝ ܕܐܠܦ ܡܪܢ
ܠܬܠܡܝܕܘ̈ܗܝ
ܐܒܘܢ ܕܒܫܡܝܐ
ܢܬܩܕܫ ܫܡܟ
ܬܐܬܐ ܡܠܟܘܬܟ
ܘܢܗܘܐ ܨܒܝܢܟ
ܐܝܟܢܐ ܕܒܫܡܝܐ
3 ܐܦ ܒܐܪܥܐ
ܘܗ̇ܒܠ ܠܚܡܐ
ܕܣܘܢܩܢ ܝܘܡܢܐ[1]
ܘܫܒܘܩ ܠܢ ܚܘ̈ܒܝܢ
ܘܚܛܗ̈ܝܢ ܐܝܟܢܐ
ܕܐܦܚܢܢ ܫܒܩܢ
ܠܚܝ̈ܒܝܢ ܘܠܐ
ܬܥܠܢ ܠܢܣܝܘܢܐ
ܐܠܐ ܦܨܢ ܡܢ
4 ܒܝܫܐ ܡܛܠ
ܕܕܝܠܟ ܗܝ
ܡܠܟܘܬܐ ܚܝܠܐ

[1] MS ܠܡ.

ܘܬܫܒܘܚܬܐ

ܠܥܠܡ ܥܠܡܝܢ

ܐܡܝܢ § **ܠܘܬܗ** § 2

ܕܐܒܘܢ ܐܕܡ

ܠܒܘܟܪܐ ܕܟܠܐ

ܡܒܪܝܢ . ܘܠܟ

5 ܫܘܡܫܝܢܐ

ܡܫܡܫܝܢ

ܕܐܢܬܘ ܡܒܣܡܝܢܐ

ܕܦܓܪ̈ܝܢ . ܘܐܢܬܘ

ܦܪܘܩ ܕܢܦܫ̈ܬܢ

ܠܘܬܐ ܕܡܠܐܟ̈ܐ § 3

ܩܕܝܫܐ ܐܠܗܐ

ܩܕܝܫܐ ܚܝܠܬܢܐ

ܩܕܝܫܐ ܠܐ ܡܝܘܬܐ

6 ܡܪܢ ܐܬܪܚܡ

ܥܠܝܢ ܡܪܢ

ܡܛܠ ܛܝܒܘܬܟ

ܡܪܢ ܐܬܪܥܐ

ܠܥܒ̈ܕܝܟ ܛܒܝܢ

ܕܩ̈ܪܐ ܗܠܝܢ ܐܡܝܢ

ܐܘܢܓܠܝܘܢ ܩܕܝܫܐ § 4

ܕܡܪܢ ܝܫܘܥ ܡܫܝܚܐ

ܟܪܘܙܘܬܐ ܕܝܘܚܢܢ

ܟܪܝܙܬ ܐܝܬܘܗܝ

ܗܘܐ ܡܠܬܐ ܘܗ̣ܘ

ܡܠܬܐ ܐܝܬܘܗܝ

. ܗܘܐ ܠܘܬ ܐܠܗܐ 7
ܘܐܠܗܐ . ܐܝܬܘܗܝ,
ܗܘܐ ܗܘ ܡܠܬܐ
ܗܢܐ ܐܝܬܘܗܝ,
ܗܘܐ ܒܪܝܫܝܬ
ܠܘܬ ܐܠܗܐ .
ܘܟܠܡܕܡ ܒܐܝܕܗ
8 ܗܘܐ ܘܒܠܥܕܘܗܝ,
ܐܦܠܐ ܚܕܐ
ܗܘܬ ܡܕܡ
ܕܗܘܐ ܒܗ
ܚܝܐ ܗܘܐ ܘܚܝܐ
ܐܝܬܝܗܘܢ ܢܘܗܪܐ
ܕܒܢܝܢܫܐ . ܘܗܘ
ܢܘܗܪܐ ܒܚܫܘܟܐ
ܡܢܗܪ ܘܚܫܘܟܐ
9 ܠܐ ܐܕܪܟܗ ܒܢܝܠ
ܕܗܘܐ ܒܫܡ ܡܠܟ
ܒܫܡܐ ܕܝܘܚܢܢ
ܗܢܐ ܐܬܐ ܠܣܗܕܘܬܐ
ܕܢܣܗܕ . ܥܠ ܢܘܗܪܐ
ܐܝܟ ܕܟܠܢܫ
ܢܗܝܡܢ, ܒܐܝܕܗ ܠܐ
ܗܘܐ ܗܘ ܢܘܗܪܐ
10 ܐܠܐ ܕܢܣܗܕ ܥܠ ܢܘܗܪܐ
ܘܢܗܘܐ ܒܥܠܡܐ
ܒܥܠܡܐ ܗܘܐ

16 ܡܢ ܦܪ̈ܕܝܣܐ
ܘܡܢܐ ܒܪܘܚܢܘܬܐ
ܘܒܗܘ ܚܝܠܐ
ܕܟܠܐ ܠܫܡܫܐ
ܘܐܘܩܦ ܠܣܗܪܐ
ܘܒܗܘܢ ܕܡܒܥ
ܠܠܐ ܐܡܝܢ
ܩܕܝܫ ܩܕܝܫ
ܩܕܝܫ ܡܪܝܐ
17 ܐܠܗܐ ܚܝܠܬܢܐ
ܕܡܠܝܢ ܫܡܝܐ
ܘܐܪܥܐ ܡܢ
ܬܫܒ̈ܚܬܗ.
ܘܡܢ ܠܘ̈ܬܗ
ܕܚܘܒܐ ܘܡܢ ܠܘ̈ܬܗ̇
ܕܡܪܬ̇ ܡܪܝܡ
ܦܓܪܢܝܬܐ ܘܕܡܪܝ
ܢܘܚܝܢ ܘܐܬܝܠܕܗ
18 ܕܡܫܝܚܐ ܢܬܒܪܟ
ܘܢܬܥܠܐ ܠܥܠܡ
ܢܘ̈ܕܐ ܗܠܝܢ ܒܗ
ܐܡܝܢ: ܘܟܕ ܐܫܠܡ
ܐܬܘܒ ܐܡܪܘ
ܘܐܡܪܘ ܕܦܪ̈ܩܢ
ܠܗ̇ ܡܠܟܘܬܐ
ܕܫܡܝܐ ܒܪ̈ܝܫܐ
ܐܝܟ ܘܝ̈ܠܕܐ

19 ܕܒܗ ܘܕܪ̈ܘܚܐ
ܐܦܘ ܡܠܟ
ܢܫܒܚܘܢ ܡܠܟ
ܗܒܘ ܘܐܒܪܘ
ܩܒܪܬܝ ܒܠܗ̇
ܒܪܬܐ ܘܐܡܢܐ
ܕܡܗܝܡܢ ܘܚܒܪܝ.
ܚܝܐ ܘܐܡܢܐ ܕܠܐ
ܡܗܝܡܢ ܡܬܚܝܒ
ܐܬܘ̈ܬܐ ܠܐܠܝܢ
20 ܕܡܗܝܡܢܝܢ
ܗܠܝܢ ܢܩܦܢ.
ܒܫܡܝ[1] ܫܐܕ̈ܐ
ܢܦܩܘܢ ܘܒܠܫܢ̈ܐ
ܚܕ̈ܬܐ ܢܡܠܠܘܢ
ܘܚܘ̈ܘܬܐ ܢܫܩܠܘܢ.
ܘܐܢ ܣܡܐ
ܕܡܘܬܐ ܢܫܬܘܢ
ܠܐ ܢܗܪܘܢ[2]
ܘܐܝܕ̈ܝܗܘܢ[3]
21 ܢܣܝܡܘܢ ܥܠ
ܟܪ̈ܝܗܝ ܘܢܬܚܠܡܘܢ.
ܟܕ ܐܡܪ ܐܬܝܗܒ
ܠܝ ܟܠ ܫܘܠܛܢ
ܒܫܡܝܐ ܘܒܐܪܥܐ
ܘܐܝܟܢܐ ܕܫܕܪܢܝ
ܐܒܝ ܐܦ ܐܢܐ

[1] MS. ܒܫܡ.
[2] MS. ܒܘܢ.
[3] MS. ܒܘܢ.

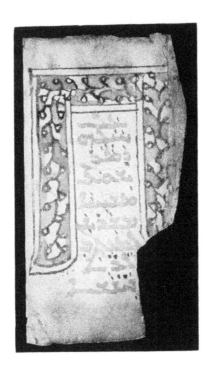

COD. B, P. 1

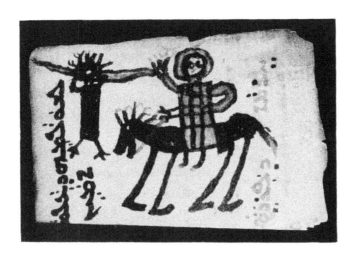

COD. B, P. 23

To face p. 42

ܡܫܕܪ ܐ̱ܢܐ ܠܟܘܢ
ܙܠܘ ܗܟܝܠ ܬܠܡܕܘ
22 ܠܟܠܗܘܢ ܥܡ̈ܡܐ
ܘܐܥܡܕܘ ܐܢܘܢ
ܒܫܡ ܐܒܐ ܘܒܪܐ
ܘܪܘܚܐ ܕܩܘܕܫܐ
ܘܐܠܦܘ ܐܢܘܢ
ܕܢܛܪܘܢ ܟܠܡܕܡ
ܕܦܩܕܬܟܘܢ [1] ܘܗܐ
ܐܢܐ ܥܡܟܘܢ ܐ̱ܢܐ
ܟܠܗܘܢ ܝܘܡ̈ܬܐ
ܥܕܡܐ
23 ܠܫܘܠܡܗ ܕܥܠܡܐ
ܐܡܝܢ

[1] In MS. ܬ omitted.

ܫܪܒܐ ܕܦܪܕܝܣܐ § 5

24 ܕܢܝܫ ܠܟܠܗܘܢ
ܒܐܪ̈ܥܐ ܘܒܡܪ̈ܘܡܐ
ܒܫܡ ܐܒܐ ܘܒܪܐ
ܘܪܘܚܐ ܕܩܘܕܫܐ
ܐܡܝܢܐ ܕܢܚ
ܡܪܝܐ ܐܠܗܐ
ܫܠܡܬܐ ܦܪܕܝܣܐ
ܒܕܢ ܘܫܡ ܒܗ
ܡܒܘܒܐ ܪܒܐ

¹ Evidently a confusion of two ideas; either we must substitute ܘܬܝܪܚ for ܠܐ ܚܡܘܢܚ, or we must add the words ܘܬܚܠܦܬܚ ܠܚ before ܡܓ ܦܝܪܚ. *See* Translation.

¹ Delete. ¹[ܕܡܒܠܠ ܘܬܒܪܝܬ̈ܘ]
² Delete. ܕܫܘܝ ܐܝ̄]² ܣܒܒܬܗܡ

ܒܗܝܡܢܘܬܗ 31
ܕܐܒܪܗܡ
ܒܕܒܝܚܘܬܗ
ܕܐܝܣܚܩ
ܒܫܠܡܘܬܐ ܕܚܝܐ
ܝܥܩܘܒ . ܒܫܘܦܪܗ
ܕܡܘܫܐ . ܒܟܗܢܘܬܐ
ܕܐܗܪܘܢ . ܒܬܘܠܘܬܐ
ܕܝܫܘܥ ܒܪܢܘܢ
ܒܛܢܢܘܬܗ ܕܦܝܢܚܣ 32
ܒܓܢܒܪܘܬܗ
ܕܝܗܘܕܐ . ܒܟܠܘܬܐ
ܕܢܒܝܐ . ܒܚܝܪܘܬܗ
ܕܫܡܘܐܝܠ ܒܡܫܡܫܢܘܬܗ
ܕܐܠܝܐ . ܒܛܢܢܗ
ܕܐܠܝܫܥ . ܒܚܙܘܐ
ܕܢܒܝܐ ܐܫܥܝܐ
ܒܗܝܟܠܐ
ܒܡܪܟܒܬܐ ܕܚܝܐ 33
ܚܙܩܝܐܝܠ ܢܒܝܐ
ܕܕܢܝܐܝܠ ܒܐܬܘܢܐ
ܕܛܠܝܐ ܒܐܕ̈ܪܐ
ܕܢܪ ܗܘܢ ܒܪ
ܡܢܗ، ܒܓܘ ܒܪܘܫܗ
ܕܝܘܢܐ . ܒܣܘܒܪܗ
ܕܗܘܫܥ . ܒܨܘܬܗ
ܕܐܪܡܝܐ ܒܟܐܒܘܬܗ
ܕܒܪܘܟ

34 ܕܐܠܗܐ ܡܠܠ ܕܝܢ
ܘܕܝܢ ܕܒܥܠܬܐ
ܡܒܪܟܝܢ ܕܡܠܐܟܗ
ܩܕܝܫܐ ܡܒܪܟ ܩܪܝܐ
ܗܘ ܗܘܡܒܪܗ ܐܢܐ . ܟܝ
ܘܟܢܫܐ ܐܪܣܪܣܬܗ ܒܪ
ܠܗ ܫܒܪ ܐܢ̈ܝܐ .
ܘܫܡܗ ܪܒܐ ܝܪܒ
ܗܝܘܕ ܕܟܠܐ ܪܒ
ܘܠܟܠܗܐ .

35 ܕܝܢ ܡܠܟ̈ܬܗ ܐܘܪܒܘܕܝܐ ܡܒܢܝܢܐ
ܕܒܫܬܒܥܬ ܘܡܗ
ܐܬܝܒܪܐ ܕܐܒܪܗܡ ܡܬܒܟܕܐ
ܗܘ ܩܒܡܗ ܘܡܒܗܬܗ
ܕܬܐܬܠܗܐ ܩܝܫܘܒ ܘܟܠܕܐܬܝ
ܚܣܘܠܡܗ
ܕܒܡܠܟܐܣ ܒܟܒܗܬܐܕܢܗ
ܘܐܘܢܪ ܐܢܟ̈ܠܝܐ . ܚܘܕܢܐ ܗܝܕ
ܘܗܕܡܐ ܐܟܪܝܐ ܕܒܪܝܥܝ
36 ܠܠܚܫܝܗܘܡ,
ܕܡܒܝܩܝܘܬܗ ܚܒܝܒܝܬܕܐ
ܕܥܠܝܐܬܐ ܘܡܥܠܐܬܠܐ
ܕܒܡܘܐ . ܐܘܡܫ̈ܐ . ܪܒܡܐ ܕܘܕܐ
ܕܒܪܕ̈ܩܝܐ
ܒܟܝܩܘܬܐ
ܕܘܗܟܐ . ܐܘܕܡܘܬ̈ܐ ܐܝܠܝܟܕܐ
ܒܩܘܠܕܘܬܐ
ܕܒܟܟܣ ܝܪܒܐ ܕܡܒܝܫܝܐ

40 ܘܡܫܝܚܢ ܘܐܚܝܓܕܐ
ܡܪܝ ܝܘܚܢܢ
ܡܥܡܕܢܐ . ܒܫܝܪ̈ܘܗܝ
ܘܕܦܛܪܘܣ
ܘܦܘܠܘܣ
ܘܐܪܒܥܐ
ܐܘܢܓܠܣ̈ܛܐ
ܡܬܝ
ܘܡܪܩܘܣ
ܘܠܘܩܐ ܘܝܘܚܢܢ
ܘܒܢܝܡܝܢ
41 ܕܡܪܝ ܬܐܘܡܐ
ܫܠܝܚܐ ܕܠܢ
ܕܒܗ ܕܦܪܘܩܢ
ܘܡܪܝ ܐܣܛܦܢܘܣ
ܒܘܟܪܐ ܕܣܗ̈ܕܐ .
ܒܡܪܝ ܕܝܘܕܘܪܘܣ
ܘܡܪܝ ܬܐܘܕܘܪܘܣ
ܘܡܪܝ ܢܣܛܘܪܝܣ
ܘܕܡܠܦ̈ܢܐ ܣܘܪ̈ܝܝܐ
ܡܪܝ ܐܦܪܝܡ
42 ܘܡܪܝ ܢܪܣܝ
ܘܡܪܝ ܐܒܪܗܡ
ܘܡܪܝ ܐܝܘܒ
ܘܡܪܝ ܥܪܒܝܠ
ܘܕܟܠܗܘܢ
ܚܒܪ̈ܝܗܘܢ ܐܡܝܢ

ܘܒܨܠܘ̈ܬܐ
ܕܐܒܗ̈ܝܢ ܪ̈ܘܚܢܝܐ .
ܐܒܐ ܦܘܠܘܣ
ܘܐܒܐ ܐܢܛܘܢܝܘܣ
ܘܐܒܐ ܡܩܪܝܣ
43 ܘܐܒܐ ܐܪܣܢܝܘܣ
ܘܐܒܐ ܐܘܓܪܝܣ
ܘܐܒܐ ܦܠܕܝܣ
ܘܐܒܐ ܐܘܪ
ܘܐܒܐ ܦܝܡܝܣ
ܘܐܒܐ ܐܡܘܢܝܐ
ܘܐܒܐ ܦܘܠܐ
ܦܫܛܐ ܘܐܒܐ
ܡܘܫܐ ܟܘܫܝܐ
ܘܐܒܐ ܦܘܪ ܛܠܠܐ
44 ܘܐܒܐ ܫܪܦܝܘܢ
ܘܐܒܐ ܡܪܩܘܣ
ܬܪܡܘܕܝܐ .
ܘܐܒܐ ܐܓܝܢܘܣ
ܘܐܒܐ ܒܪܘܢܝܘܣ
ܘܐܒܐ ܫܪܡܝܛܐ
ܘܕܟܠܗܘܢ
ܚܒܪ̈ܝܗܘܢ
ܐܡܝܢ . ܘܒܨܠܘ̈ܬܗܘܢ
ܕܡܢ̈ܚܢܐ ܘܡܟܬ̈ܪܢܐ
ܡܪܝ ܐܘܓܝܢ
45 ܘܡܪܝ ܫܠܝܛܐ

ܘܡܪܝ ܣܪܓܝܣ
ܘܡܪܝ ܒܟܘܣ
ܘܡܪܝ ܫܡܥ
ܘܡܪܝ ܒܘܢܝܐ
ܘܡܪܝ ܐܘܓܝܢܐ
ܘܡܪܝ ܒܒܕܐ
ܘܬܬܘܣ ܘܡܪܝ
ܝܘܣܦ ܕܝܘܕܒܠ
ܘܡܪܝ ܕܢܝܐ
ܘܡܪܝ ܒܒܝ
46 ܕܫܡܥܐ . ܘܡܪܝ
ܣܪܓܝܣ ܕܘܪܐ
ܘܡܪܝ ܒܘܕܘܗܝ
ܕܒܝܬ ܚܠܐ
ܘܡܪܝ ܡܘܢ
ܕܐܢܒܪ . ܘܡܪܝ
ܫܡܥܘܢ ܕܐܦܡܝܐ
ܘܡܪܝ ܒܪܥܠ
ܕܦܪܣܐ . ܘܡܪܝ
ܒܪܘܢܐ . ܘܡܪܝ
47 ܢܒܘܒ ܡܥܡܘܕܢܐ .
ܘܡܪܝ ܥܒܘܪ
ܘܡܪܝ ܡܘܪܛܐ
ܘܐܚܕܐ ܕܕܝܪܐ
ܕܒܪܐ . ܘܫܡܘܢܝ
ܘܒܢܝܗ ܘܡܫܡܫܢܝܬܐ
ܘܬܪܝܢ ܒܢܝܗ

ܘܡܪܝ ܣܗ̈ܕܐ

ܘܡܪܝ ܡܪܘܬܐ

ܘܐܚܘܗ̇ܝ ܕܐܒܘܗ̇

48 ܘܡܒܪܟܠܠܐ ܕܕܘܟܝܢܐ

ܘܡܪܝ ܒܪܫܒܬܝ

ܘܡܪܝ ܫܡܥܘܢ

ܕܝܠܢܐ . ܘܡܪܝ

ܫܡܫܘ . ܘܡܪܝ

ܠܒܘܪܝܫ . ܘܣܗ̈ܕܐ

ܕܟܘܪܐ ܕܚܝܫ .

ܘܡܪܝ ܒܪܚܕܒܫܒܐ

ܘܡܪܝ ܒܪܨܘ̈ܡܐ

ܘܡܪܝ ܐܠܝܐ

49 ܘܡܪܝ ܓܒܪܝܠ

ܘܡܪܝ ܡܝܟܐܝܠ

ܘܪܒܢ ܗܘܪܡܙܕ .

ܘܡܪܝ ܝܥܩܘܒ

ܕܒܝܬ ܥܒ̈ܐ . ܘܪܒܢ

ܦܬܝܘܢ ܕܕܝܪ . ܘܪܒܢ

ܝܘܣܦ ܚܙܝܐ

ܘܡܪܝ ܦܪܕܓ

ܘܡܪܝ ܦܠ̈ܛܐ

ܘܡܪܝ ܒܒܕܫܘܒ

50 ܢܘܪܝܦܬܐ . ܘܡܪܝ

ܥܠܝܦܬܐ ܕܕܝܫܝܢܐ

ܘܡܪܝ ܝܘܣܦ

ܘܪܒܢ ܐܗܪܘܢ

ܘܡܪܝ ܦܦܐ ܘܡܪܝ
ܫܒܐ ܐܫܝܐ. ܘܡܪܝ
ܝܒܘܪܐ. ܘܡܪܝ
ܩܘܡܐ. ܘܡܪܝ
ܕܘܡܛܝܢܐ
ܘܡܪܝ ܕܘܡܛ
51 ܘܡܪܝ ܐܚܐ. ܘܡܪܝ
ܚܢܢܐ. ܘܡܪܝ
ܐܒܪܗܡ ܡܒܪܝܐ
ܘܡܪܝ ܡܘܪܣܡܘܣ
ܓܠܝܐ ܘܐܡܗ
ܡܪܬܝ ܡܠܝܬܐ
ܘܡܪܝ ܝܚܐ. ܘܡܪܝ
ܒܢܝܐ. ܘܡܪܝ
ܥܒܕܝܫܘܥ
ܘܡܪܝ ܬܡܣܛܣ
52 ܘܡܪܝ ܒܘܒܒܐ
ܘܡܪܝ ܚܘܫܐ
ܒܠܘܬܗ
ܕܡܪܝ ܝܘܚܢ
ܡܗܡܕܢܐ.
ܘܡܪܝ ܝܘܚܢ
ܐܘܪܗܝܛܐ
ܘܡܪܝ ܝܘܚܢ
ܕܠܘܬܦܪܐ. ܘܡܪܝ
ܝܘܚܢ ܚܙܝܐ
53 ܘܡܪܝ ܝܘܚܢ

ܐܚܝܟ . ܘܡܪܝ

ܘܫܡ ܐܩܦܪܝܟ

ܘܡܪܝ . ܘܫܡ ܕܠܢܝܟ

ܘܡܪܝ . ܘܫܡ

ܣܪܟܛܠܟ . ܘܡܪܝ

ܟܘܝܢܟ . ܘܡܪܝ

ܘܫܡ ܒܪ ܚܠܩܝܟ .

ܘܡܪܝ . ܘܫܡ

ܒܪ ܘܗܒܪ

ܘܡܪܝ . ܘܫܡ

ܘܡܪܝ . ܐܦܠܪܝ ܒܪ 54

ܘܫܡ ܒܪ ܢܘܡܝ

ܘܡܪܝ . ܘܫܡ

ܕܣܚܪܬܐ . ܘܡܪܝ

ܘܫܡ ܡܒܟܐ . ܘܡܪܝ

ܘܫܡ ܕܐܟܒܪ

ܘܡܪܝ . ܘܫܡ

ܕܒܠܩܡ . ܘܡܪܝ

ܘܫܡ ܕܐܢܝܠ

ܘܡܪܝ . ܘܫܡ

ܕܣܠܟܐ . ܘܡܪܝ

ܐܠܟ ܪܠܝܚ ܐܟܣܘܬܝܢ 55

ܘܡܪܝ ܫܒܠܬ

ܐܟܐ . ܘܚܣܒ

ܚܠܘܢ ܟܕܐܪܐ

ܘܘܢܟܩܝ ܘܡܩܪܬܐ

ܕܚܠܡ ܫܒܪܐ ܘܡܪܐ

57

59 ܠܦܘܒܝܢܬܐ
ܐܒܘܗ ܕܡܫܝܚܐ
ܦܪܘܩܢ ܘܡܚܝܢܢ.
ܒܒܪܝܐ ܕܚܕܬܐ
ܗܘܬ ܡܢ ܠܦܘܪܐ
ܕܒܪܝܢ. ܘܡܢ ܟܠ
ܦܪܕܝܣܐ ܘܐܬܬ
ܠܐܘܪܫܠܡ ܡܕܝܢܬܐ
ܘܡܢ ܒܐܠ ܗܘܐ
60 ܡܪܢ ܐܬܐ ܘܠ
ܥܒܪܐ ܘܠܘ̈ܕܐ
ܕܡܕܒܚܝܢ
ܘܡܚܝܢ ܘܐܡܪܝܢ
ܐܘܫܥܢܐ
ܒܡܪ̈ܘܡܐ.
ܐܘܫܥܢܐ ܠܒܪܗ
ܕܕܘܝܕ ܒܪܝܟ
ܕܐܬܐ ܒܫܡܗ
61 ܕܡܪܝܐ. ܘܒܢ̈ܫܐ
ܟܠܗܘܢ ܠܒܝܫܝܢ
ܗܘܘ ܫܘ̈ܒܚܐ
ܕܐܝ̈ܠܢܐ ܘܡܕܝܚܝܢ
ܗܘܘ ܠܡܪܢ ܟܕ
ܪܟܝܒ ܗܘܐ ܥܠ
ܥܝܠܐ ܡܟܒܫܐ
ܘܡܕܒܪ ܗܘܐ
ܡܢ ܒܢ̈ܫܐ

I

71

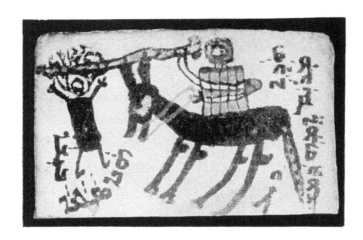

Cod. B, p. 57

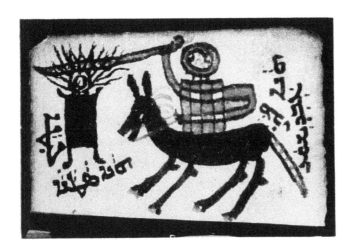

Cod. B, p. 71

To face p. 60

ܗܿܝ ܒܫܥܬܐ
ܘܦܠܓܘܬܐ ܐܣܦܪܗ̇
ܘܐܚܪܬܗ̇
ܘܫܬܡܗ̇ ܘܐܡܝܪ
ܠܗ̇ ܕܠܐ ܫܠܝܛ
ܠܟ ܕܬܫܘܐ
ܚܝܠܟ ܘܓܢܒܪܘܬܟ
80 ܘܡܣܒܪܘܬܟ
ܒܒܢܝܗ ܕܐܠܗܐ
ܚܙܐ ܠܟܝܢ
ܗ̈ܕܐ ܗܠܝܢ
ܘܬܘܒ ܡܒܘܥܐ
ܠܟ ܒܗ̇ܘ
ܕܗܘܝܢ ܡܢܗ
ܡܠܐ̈ܟܐ ܘܒܢ̈ܝܢܫܐ
ܕܐܝܟ ܐܝܬ ܠܟ
ܫܡܗ̈ܐ
81 ܐ̱ܚܪ̈ܢܐ ܟܠ ܠܝ
ܘܚܘܝ ܠܝ ܘܠܐ
ܬܟܣܐ ܡܢܝ
ܡܢܕܡ ܐܡܪܐ ܠܗ
ܟܠܢܐ ܐ̱ܢܐ ܠܟ
ܒܕ ܠܐ ܓܢܝܐ .
ܐܝܬ ܠܝ ܫܡܗ̈ܐ
ܐ̱ܚܪ̈ܢܐ ܬܪܥܣܪ
ܕܟܠܗܝܢ ܕܟܬܝܒ
ܠܗܘܢ ܘܬܠܝܐ

86

K

ܠܐ ܐܬܡܗܬ ¹ ܠܐ

¹ MS. ܐܬܡܘܗܬ.

ܫܪܝܪܬܐ
ܡܢ ܒܝܬ ܓܢܙܗ
ܕܫܡܝܢ ܚܝ̈ܠܘܬܐ
ܕܢ̈ܒܝܐ
ܘܬܫܒܘܚܬܐ
94 ܕܫ̈ܠܝܚܐ
ܘܒܫܪܟܗ
ܕܡܪܝ ܓܘܪܓܝܣ
ܣܗܕܐ ܢܨܝܚܐ
ܘܕܡܪܝ ܫܡܥܘܢ
ܟܐܦܐ ܘܕܡܪܝ
ܒܢܝ ܘܕܡܪܝ
ܡܘܦܪܢܐ
ܘܡܪܝ ܣܣܡ
95 ܘܕܟܠܗܘܢ
ܣܗܕ̈ܘܗܝ
ܘܩܕ̈ܝܫܘܗܝ
ܕܡܪܢ ܠܥܠܡ
ܥܠܡܝܢ ܐܡܝܢ

ܕܚܢܢܐ ܒܣܝܡܬܐ § 9
96 **ܘܡܫܚܬܐ**
ܚܢܢܐ ܒܣܝܡܬܐ
ܢܦܩܬ ܡܢ ܚܢܢܐ
ܕܠܒܐ ܘܦܓܪ
ܒܗ ܒܥܓܠ
ܡܠܐܟܐ ܘܐܡܪ
ܠܗ ܠܐܒܐ

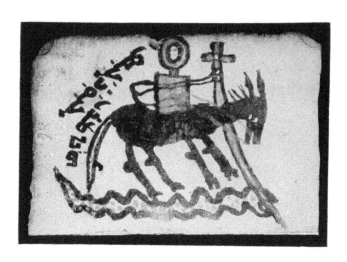

COD. B, P. 86

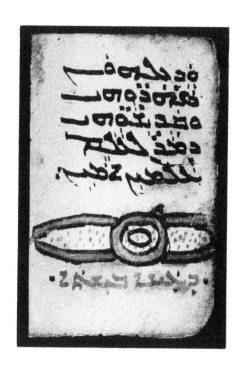

COD. B, P. 95

To face p. 68

ܐܝܠܐ ܐܢܬܝ ܐܘ
ܒܪܬ ܐܒܕܢܐ
97 ܐܡܪܐ ܠܗ ܐܝܠܐ
ܐ̇ܢܐ ܠܡܫܚܠܦ
ܓܒܪ̈ܐ ܘܢܫ̈ܐ
ܘܛ̈ܠܝܐ ܘܛ̈ܠܝܬܐ
ܘܢܩ̈ܒܬܐ ܕܕܟܪ̈ܐ
ܘܕܦܪܫܬܐ ܐܡܪ̈
ܠܗ̇ ܓܒܪܝܠ
ܡܠܐܟܐ ܠܐ
98 ܟܠܗ̇ ܠܦܪܕܝܣܐ
ܘܠܐ ܚܙܬܗ̇
ܠܐܠܗܐ ܪܒܐ
ܗ̇ܘ ܕܐܠܦ
ܐܠܦ̈ܝܢ ܘܪܒܘ
ܪ̈ܒܘܢ ܕܡܠܐ̈ܟܐ
ܕܪܚܡܝܢ ܠܗ
ܒܥܡܗ ܐܣܝܢ
ܠܝ ܘܐܣܪܢܐ
99 ܠܟܝ ܐܘ ܟܝܢܐ
ܒܥܬܐ ܘܫܡܫܬܐ
ܟܝܢܐ ܕܢܘܗܪ̈ܐ
ܘܟܝܢܐ ܕܟܢ̈ܬܐ
ܘܟܝܢܐ ܕܪ̈ܘܚܐ
ܘܟܝܢܐ ܕܡܪ̈ܟܒܐ
ܘܟܝܢܐ ܢܘܗܪܬܐ
ܘܟܝܢܐ ܙܪܘܚܬܐ

101 ܐܠܚܬܡ ܚܠܠܡܗ (sic)

§ 10

[1] Delete ܐܘܗܝ.
[2] MS. ܒܪܐܝܫܢܘܩ.
[3] Supply the words ܫ̈ܘܪܐ ܡܠܝܢ.
[4] MS. ܠܒܐ.

ܐܦܪܢܐ ܠܟܘܢ
ܒܗ̇ܘ ܡܠܐܟܐ
106 ܕܕܐܢ ܐܢܬܬܐ
ܕܦܪܘܢܐ ܪܒܢܗ̇
ܒܡܚܠܝ ܚܕ
ܒܒܟܐ ܘܕܝܢܐ.
ܐܠܐ ܢܬܠܘܢ
ܐܝܟ ܬܢܝܢܐ
ܡܢ ܗܕܡ ܟܠܟܠܐ
ܠܟܠܡ ܟܠܡܚܡ
ܐܡܚܡ. § **ܕܒܪܬ** § 11
ܦܓܪܐ
107 ܒܫܡ ܐܒܐ
ܘܒܪܐ ܘܪܘܚܐ
ܕܩܘܕܫܐ ܡܪܝܐ
ܐܠܗܐ ܚܝܠܬܢܐ
ܐܣܝ ܟܠ. ܐܢܬ
ܟܪ ܐܡܪܬ
ܒܡܒܪܬܟ
ܕܟܠ ܕܢܐܠ
ܢܦܒ ܘܕܒܒܐ
108 ܡܫܒܚ ܬܫܒܘܚ
ܠܗ ܐܦ ܗܫܐ
ܡܪܝܐ ܐܠܗܐ
ܚܝܠܬܢܐ ܘܫܒܚܐ
ܐܢܐ ܡܢܟ ܡܬܠ
ܒܒܢܟ ܕܬܠܚܡ

¹ ܕܫܝ̈ܝܐ ܘܕܐܘܣ̈ܝܐ¹

² ܘܪܘܚ̈ܐ ܘܩܝ̈ܝܐ

¹ MS. ܪܕܝܘܣܝܐܕ.

² Re spelling of last two terms, *cf.* C, § 3 (note).

L

ܐܣܝܪ ܒܫܡܝܐ
ܗܟܢܐ ܡܪܝܐ
ܐܠܗܐ ܫܠܝܛܐ
ܐܣܪܢܐ ܘܡܫܪܝܢܐ
ܘܛܪܕܢܐ
ܘܡܫܒܩܢܐ
ܠܡܠܟ̈ܐ
115 ܘܫ̈ܘܠܛܢܐ
ܘܐܡܝܪ̈ܐ
ܘܗܓܡ̈ܘܢܐ
ܘܡܢܛ̈ܘܢܐ
ܘܕܝ̈ܢܐ
ܘܦܩ̈ܝܕܐ
ܘܦܩ̈ܘܕܐ
ܘܓܒܪ̈ܐ
ܘܢܫ̈ܐ ܕܠܐ
ܢܬܡܠܠܘܢ
116 ܕܒܫ ܘܕܣܢܐ
ܒܫܡܗ ܕܠܚܝܢ
ܬ̈ܘܕܐ ܗܠܝܢ
ܒܗ̇ܘ ܫܠܐ
ܘܒܗ̇ܘ ܠܒܘܫܐ
ܕܠܒܝܫ ܗܘܐ
ܐܠܒܫܝܪܘܗ
ܒܪ ܦܠܓܘܗ
ܗ̇ܘ ܕܒܒܫܗ̇
ܠܐܪܒܐ

117 ܟܠܗ̇ ܗܕܝܢܐ
ܡܪܝܐ ܐܠܗܐ
ܫܠܝܛܐ
ܠܒܫ ܓܒܝܢ
ܬܘܕܐ ܗܠܝܢ
ܠܒܘܫܐ ܕܐܒܘܬܐ
ܘܕܦܘܪܩܢܐ
ܘܕܩ ܡܠܟ̈ܐ
ܘܡܪ̈ܐ ܘܫܘ̈ܠܛܢܐ
ܘܐܡܚܝ̈ܐ ܘܕܝ̈ܢܐ
118 ܐܡܝܢ ܘܐܡܝܢ :
* ܫ[ܠܡ]ܬ ܟܬܝ[ܒܬܐ]
[ܗܕܐ ܒܐܝ]ܕ̈ܝ
[ܡܚܝܠ]ܐ
ܕܢܐܠ
ܒܪ ܡܫܚܐ
ܒܘܫܒܐ
ܐܠܘܫܢܐ
ܘܠܗ ܫܘܒ :[1]

[1] Short for ܫܘܒܚܐ.

* The letters enclosed [ ] are added by conjecture, the MS. being torn in these places.

ܗܡ ܐܠܗܐ ܗܚܡܝ ܐܠܟܝܐ [or ܕܢܝܘܝܒܐ[3]] ܒܕܪܐ ܕܪ̈ܬܐ ܕܦܠܠܐ
ܘܠ ܒܕܪܟܐ ܬܚܘܕܐ[4] (sic) ܫܥܡ ܝܢ ܡܪܚܕ ܒܪܪܘ ܢܒܕ ܝܚܣ
ܡܥܠܟܐ[6] (sic) ܒܪܕܝܐ ܘܡܣܒܐ ܬܣܬܡ ܘܡܛܘܕܐ ܘܒܝܕ̈ܘܪ ܕܠܝܒܐܪ
---

[1] Evidently so. I would state, once for all, that the sign of the
plural is not always marked in this MS.

[2] Or ܕܒܐܥܪܝ.   [3] MS. ܪܢܝܘܝܒܐ.   [4] l. ܢܚܬܘܕܐ.

[5] l. ܕܠܚܝܪܐ.   [6] l. ܥܠܟܐ.

[7] The passage beginning ܕܠܟܘܬ ܪܚܝܬ till ܘܕܠܚܘܬܐ is
underlined in the original.

ܪܘܠܟܕ݂ܟܐ ܪܠܬܝܐ ܪܠܦܡܐ ܪܬܢ ܚܬ ܪܬܐܡܢ ܦܝܕ݂ܗܡ ܥܚܡ
ܕܝܐܪ ܪܐܘܝܝܐ ܪܡܡܘܐ ܚܬ݁ܬ ܪܠܐ ܕܘܠ ܚܣܝܐ ܚܘ ܒܘܚܬܐ ܦܣܡܝ
ܕܢܪ ܡܢ ܕܬܚ ܡܚܘ ܕܝܠܚܝ ܡܘܐ ܪܘܢܐ ܡܠܡ ܗܠܐ ܪܚܕܡ

ܪܝܘܡܐ ܪܠܝܠܐ ܪܒܘܥܠܝܟܐ §3

ܒܥܕ ܐܪܟ ܡܣܐ ܩܝܕܐ ܘܐܘܢܐ ܪܐܕܣܐ : ܒܥܕ ܠܟ݂ܝܕܝ

(remaining Syriac text)

---

[1] Similarly, the passage beginning ܠܟ݂ܝܕܝ till ܕܝܪܚܠ is underlined.

[2] The words from ܒܕܝܪܚܠ till ܡܒܝܪܚܠ are underlined.

[3] ܝ omitted in MS.

§ 5 ܐܡܪܐ ܕܝܢ ܕܥܘܒܐ (sic) ܕܡܚܝܢ
 [2] ܒܝܬܐ

ܐܡܪ ܐܠܐ ܒܪܐ ܘܐܘܢܐ ܕܡܩܒܘܬܐ ܒܡܠܬܗ ܘܐܡܪ ܕܝܢ ܩܫ ܗܢ ܕܝܢ، ܥܠܠܝܐ، ܕܝܢ، ܘܥܠܝ ܘܡܕܪܕܬܝܗ ܩܘܪܒܐ ܘܡܚܐ ܘܚܫܝܒܬܐ ܠܟܘܠܗܘܢ ܐܝܟ ܣܘܘ ܘܒܪܐ ܗܘ ܚܝܐ ܕܒܬܪܬܝܢ ܫܡܥ ܒܝܬܐ ܐܪ݁ܐ ܒܐܠܦܐ ܡܪܘܬܐ ܘܡܪܐ ܗܘ ܕܠܡܚܒܬ ܡܪܐ ܐܪܘܪܐ ܕܒ ܗ ܗܘ ܗܘܐ ܕܥܘܒܐ ܠ ܟܠ ܕܥܘܒܐ ܗܘܐ ܚܝܐ ܠ ܟܘܠ ܚܝܐ ܥܠ [3] ܗܘܪܐܢ ܕܡܚܒܬܐ ܥܠ ܚܝܐ ܠ ܚܝܐ [l. ܗܕܐ] ܗܕܐ ܕܠܝܐ ܕܝܐ ܕܝܐ، ܕܝܢ ܡܒܘܬܐ ܘܠܒܝܬܐ ܕܝܢ، ܣܡܠ ܐܡܪ

---

[1] Or ܗܝܡܝܘܢ.

[2] The MS. is indistinct; ܕܡܚܝܢ ܘܒܝܬܐ might be meant.

[3] Seems so; the MS. is not clear; ܗܘܪܐ would suit better.

§ 6 ܡܠܚܐ ܕܢܦܠܐ ܒܚܠܐ

ܒܫܡ ܐܒܐ ܘܒܪܐ ܘܪܘܚܐ ܕܩܘܕܫܐ ܦܘܩ ܡܠܚܐ
ܡܢ ܓܘ ܚܠܐ ܗܠܝܢ ܕܦ ܒܪ ܦ ܐܝܟ ܕܢܦܩܘ ܒ̈ܢܝ
ܝܣܪܝܠ ܠܡܕܒܪܐ ܒܝܕ ܡܘܫܐ ܢܒܝܐ ܐܝܟ ܕܢܦܩ ܐܕܡ
ܡܢ ܦܪܕܝܣܐ ܗܘܢ[1] ܕܢܝܐܝܠ ܡܢ ܓܘܒܐ ܚܢܢܝܐ ܡܢ
ܐܬܘܢܐ ܕܢܘܪܐ ܢܘܚ ܡܢ ܩܒܘܬܐ ܗܟܢܐ ܘܠܡܠܚܐ
ܦܘܩ ܡܢ ܓܘ ܚ̈ܠܐ ܗܠܝܢ ܕܦ ܒܪ ܦ ܒܐܠܗܐ ܚ̈ܝܐ
ܡܫܝܚܐ ܐܡܝܢ ܐ̇ܡܝܢ

§ 7 ܬܘܠܥܐ[2] ܕܗܘܝܢ ܒܪܢܫܐ

ܒܪܝܟ ܟܠ ܒܦܘܪܐ ܕܫܘܠܛܢܐ ܥܥܝ ܟܠ ܬܘܠ̈ܥܐ[2]
ܬܘܠܥܐ[2] ܢܦܠܝܢ ܒܡܫܚܐ ܒܪܝܟ ܟܦܘܪܐ ܒܫܡܗ ܕܡܪܢ
ܝܫܘܥ ܡܫܝܚܐ ܘܕܓܒܪܝܠ ܪܝܫܗ ܕܡܠܐܟܐ ܘܪ̈ܒܢܐ
ܠܗܦܟ ܡܢܐ[3] ܫܠܐ ܥܕ ܘܫܠܐ ܫܓ̣ܕ ܘܠܐ ܒܟܥ
ܓܕ̈ܝܫܐ ܗܟܢܐ ܠܐ ܢܫܘܟܘܢ ܬܘܠܥܐ ܒܦܠܢ ܒܪ
ܦܠܢ ܐܘ ܒܥ̈ܝܪܐ ܐܘ ܬܘܪܐ ܒܫܡ ܫ̈ܢܝܐ ܚ̈ܫܝܢܐ
ܐܡܝܢ ܐܡܢ

§ 8 ܐܣܘܪܐ ܕܢܘܪܐ ܡܢ ܒܘܪܟܐ

ܒܪܝܟ ܟܠ ܡܢܗ[4] ܒܫܡ ܐܒܐ ܘܒܪܐ ܘܪܘܚܐ
ܕܩܘܕܫܐ: ܐܣܪܢܐ ܠܗ ܢܘܪܐ ܗܢܐ ܒܘܪܟܐ ܗܢܐ
ܘܠܢܘܪܐ ܗܢܐ ܦ̇ܠܣܛܝܢܐ ܗܢܐ ܕܠܐ ܠܗܘܐ ܘܠܐ ܠܗܠܐ

[1] *See* Translation. The MS. has ܗܘ ܠܡ.

[2] In the MS. the word looks like ܬܘܠܠܐ; but judging from the conclusion in which it occurs as ܬܘܠܥܐ, we are justified in reading as above. (*Cf.* Appendix, B. M. § 65.)

[3] Is this ܠܗܦܟܐ, ܐܗܦܟܐ or ܐܗܦܟ̈ܐ?

[4] The heading is here repeated in the original; evidently an error.

---

[1] Short for ܘܩܝ̈ܒܠܐ.   [2] This seems to be the word as written.

ܠܗܘܢ ܡܫܝܪܝܐ ܠܗܘܢ ܐܝܟ ܣܘܣܝܐ ܒܠܓܡܐ
ܐܝܟ .. ܐܝܟ ܬܘܪܐ ܒܢܝܪܐ ܐܝܟ ܡܚܝܬܐ ܒܡܒܥܪܐ
ܐܝܟ ܒܦܚܒܐ ܒܥܡܩܐ ܐܝܟ ܢܘܢܐ ܒܡܝܐ ܐܣܘܪ ܠܗ
ܒܠܫܡܕܐ[1] ܕܡܢ ܥܡܟܐ ܢܦܠ ܒܠ ܒܠ[2] ܦܘܡܚܝܗܘܢ ܘܒܠ
ܠܥܝܢܝܗܘܢ ܕܒܢܝܢܫܐ ܒܢܫܐ ܘܢܫܡܬܐ ܐܡܝܪܬܐ ܡܠܟܐ
ܘܕܝܢܐ ܥܠܝܬܢܐ ܠܠܘܩܒܐ ܥܡܝܐ ܦܘܩܕܐ ܐܝܟܢܐ ܒܫܡ
ܓܒܪܝܠ ܡܝܟܐܝܠ ܒܫܡ ܪܘܦܐܝܠ ܒܫܡ ܐܗܝܐ ܐܫܪܗܝܐ
ܐܠܫܕܝ، ܐܕܘܢܝ ܡܪܝܐ ܨܒܐܘܬ ܐܣܘܪܐ ܦܘܡܝܗܘܢ
ܘܠܥܝܢܝܗܘܢ ܕܒܢܝܢܫܐ ܒܢܫܐ ܠܠܘܩܒܐ ܘܚܝܘܬܐ ܘܕܝܢܐ
ܒܠܗܘܢ ܒܢܝܢܫܐ ܒܢܝܫܐ ܘܢܫܡܬܐ ܕܡ ܠܓܒܝܢ ܢܦܪܐ
ܗܠܝܢ ܒܢܝܢܗ ܫܢܝܐ ܕܐܝܠܝܢܐ ܡܪܝܐ ܘܐܠܗܐ ܒܫܡ
ܐܒܐ ܥܙܪܐ ܐܡܝܢ

§ 11 ܐܣܘܪܐ ܕܐܫܪ̈ܝܐ[3] ܐܣܘܪܐ ܕܠܒܝܐ

ܒܫܡ ܐܒܐ ܘܒܪܐ ܘܪܘܚܐ ܕܩܘܕܫܐ ܐܪܓܠ ܕܪܓܠ
ܒܪܓܠ ܙܪܓܠ ܫܪܓܠ ܗܪܓܠ[4] ܥܒܕܐ ܕܐܪܐ ܡܦܠܝܢܐ
ܘܡܣܪܘܦܝܣ ܐܦܪܘܕ ܢܦܠܝܐ ܥܠܝܗܘܢ ܦܪܝܣ[5] ܘܥܡܥܐ
ܘܢܗܪܐ ܗܘ ܢܗܘܐ ܒܡ ܠܓܒܝܢ ܡܘܕܐ ܗܠܝܢ ܐܡܒܢܐ
ܕܝܫܡ ܐܠܗܐ ܠܡܒܥܐ ܪܥܗ ܕܒܒܪܝܗ (*sic*) ܐܡܒܢܐ
ܕܝܫܡ ܐܠܗܐ ܠܕܘܪ ܐܡܒܢܐ ܕܝܫܡ ܐܠܗܐ ܠܕܢܝܐܝܠ
ܢܒܝܐ

[1] Perhaps ܒܫܪܒܐ should be read. [2] Delete.

[3] MS. ܕܐܫܝ̈ܪܐ.

[4] The words from ܒܫܡ ܐܒܐ till ܗܪܓܠ are underlined in MS.

[5] It is very questionable whether this version of the last six or seven words as in our MS. is correct; *cf.* Appendix, B. M. § 55, where the variation is remarkable and interesting. *See* note to Translation.

§ 12 ܒܪܘܩܐ ܕܚܨܐ

ܒܫܡ ܐܒܐ ܘܒܪܐ ܕܩܘܕ: ܒܫܡ ܐܠܗ̈ܐ ܚܝ̈ܐ
ܬܘܩܦܐ ⁘ ܡܚܢܢܐ ܡܪܚܡܢܐ ܐܝܬܝܐ
ܒܪ̈ܚܡܝܟ ܦܘ̈ܩܕܢܐ ܡܫܬܡ ܒܡܪܚܡܢܘܬܟ ܐܡܪܬ
ܠܥܡܐ ܘܫܠܚܬ ܘܓܐܬ ܡܪܝ، ܒܫܠܝܟ ܙܒܢܐ ܬܘܩܦܐ
ܘܒܠܗ[1] ܕܟܠ ܡܪܝ، ܫܬܘܩ ܢܐ ܠܫܒܩܠܐ ܗ̈ܢܐ ܡܢܪܐ
ܘܡܢ ܚܨܐ ܡܢ ܕܦܘܢܐ ܕܦ ܒܪ ܦ ܡܢ ܠܗܬ ܡܪܬܗ، ܡܪܬܡ
ܠܒܝܫܬܐ ܐܡܝܢ ܦ̇ܡܝܢ ܐܡܝܢ

§ 13 ܐܣܘܪܐ ܕܥܩܪܬܐ

ܒܫܡ ܐܒܐ ܘܒܪܐ ܘܪܘܚܐ ܕܩܘܕܫܐ ܐܣܘܪܐ ܠܗ
ܥܩܪܬܐ ܕܦܠܢ ܒܪ ܦܠܢ ܒܕܘܪܐ ܠܐ ܘܠܕܐ ܠܟܠܗ ܒܕܘܟܬܐ
ܐܝܟ ܬܘܪܐ ܒܢܝܪܐ ܐܝܟ ܡܫܚܬܐ ܒܡܒܪܐ ܐܝܟ ܢܘܢܐ
ܒܝܡܐ ܐܝܟ ܫܘܫܢܐ ܒܦܨܘܬܐ[2] ܐܝܟ ܒܨܠܐ
ܒܡܫܒܚܐ ܐܝܟ ܒܘܒܒܒܐ (sic) ܒܠܦܘܢܐ ܕܫܒܒܐ (sic)
ܐܝܟ ܐܝܠܢܐ ܕܢܨܝܒܝܢ ܒܐܪܥܐ ܗܟܢܐ ܐܣܘܪܐ ܠܗ
ܥܩܪܬܐ ܕܦܠܢ ܒܪ ܦܠܢ ܒܫܡܗ ܚ̈ܝܐ ܕܐܨܠܒܐ ܐܡܝܢ

§ 14 ܐܣܘܪܐ ܕܐܒܐ ܡܢ ܩܢܝܢܐ

ܒܫܡ ܐܒܐ ܘܒܪܐ ܘܪܘܚܐ ܕܩܘܕ: ܨܠܘܬܐ ܘܒܥܘܬܐ
ܕܡܪܝ، ܕܢܝܐܝܠ ܢܒܝܐ ܙܒܢܐ ܒܒܒܝܠܐ ܕܫܕܘ ܠܓܘܒܐ
ܕܐܪ̈ܝܐ ܠܓ ܘܗܡ ܒܦܘܪܐ ܡܢ ܠܗܬܐ ܘܐܡܪ ܡ̈ܪܝܐ
ܐܠܗܐ ܫܠܝܬܐ ܒܒܢܐ ܡ̈ܠܝܟ ܟܠ ܒܢܝܐ ܕܢܬܒܪ[3]
ܫܡܥܝܢ ܡܪܝܐ ܡܪܝ، ܝܫܘܥ ܡܫܝܚܐ ܘܫܡ ܕܠ ܠܐ ܕܢܝܐܝܠ
ܘܠܐ ܢܐܬܘܢ ܕܐܒܐ ܘܕܒܐ ܘܢܡܪܐ ܘܚܝ̈ܘܬܐ ܠܥܢܐ

[1] Perhaps for ܘܒܟܠܐ. [2] l. ܒܦܨܘܕܬܐ. [3] l. ܕܢܬܕܒܪ.

ܕܐܠܗܝܢ ܥܘܕܪܐ ܗܠܝܢ ܠܚܬܡܬܐ ܦܓܪ̈ܝܗܘܢ ܘܠܢܦܫ̈ܬܗܘܢ
ܘܠܒܢ̈ܝܗܘܢ ܕܐܒܐ ܘܕܒܐ ܘܡܪ̈ܥܝܬܐ ܡܢ ܟܐ̈ܒܐ ܡܢ ܟܠܗ
ܡܢ ܬܘܪܐ ܕܐܠܗܝܢ ܥܘ̈ܕܪܐ ܗܠܝܢ ܐܡܝܢ

ܐܣܘܪܐ ܕܟܠܒܐ § 15

ܒܫܡ ܐܒܐ ܘܒܪܐ ܕܩܘܕ: ܡܪܝܫ [ܘ]ܡܪ̈ܝܢ ܒܐܘܪ[1]
ܐܝܠܝܢ ܗܘܘ[2] ܘܐܡܪܢܬ ܡܪܝܫ ܠܡܪ̈ܝܢ ܘܗܘܐ ܐܬܬܐ ܠܝ
ܟܠܒܐ ܘܐܡܪܝܢ ܡܪ̈ܝܢ ܠܡܪܝܫ ܗܐ ܐܣܘܪܐ ܗܦܟ ܐܢܐ
ܠܗܘܢ ܒܟ̈ܠܒܐ ܕܦܪܙܠܐ ܘܒܟ̈ܐܦܐ ܕܢܚ̈ܫܐ ܘܦܪܙܠܐ
ܚܠܦ ܢܒܚܬܗܘܢ (sic) ܘܒܣܘܦܪ (sic) ܪ̈ܓܠܝܗܘܢ[3] (sic) ܕܟܠܒܐ[4]
ܗܠܝܢ ܕܟܣܝܢ ܘܠܐ ܢܒܣܝ ܘܠܐ ܡܠܟܝܢ ܕܐܠܗܝܢ ܥܘܕܪܐ
ܗܠܝܢ ܘܠܐ ܟܣܝܢ

ܡܠܒܫܘܬܐ ܕܒܪܫܐ § 16

ܒܫܡ ܐܒܐ ܘܒܪܐ ܘܪܘܚܐ ܕܩܘ: ܒܫܡ ܦܘܩܐ ܡܪܝ
ܦܘܩ: ܡܪܝ ܢܦܘܩܐ ܡܪܝ، ܦܘܩܐ ܐܢܬ ܡܠܒܫܘ[5] ܕܒܪܫܐ
ܦܘܩ ܡܢ ܒܣܪܐ ܕܦܠܢ ܒܪܗ ܕܦܠܢ ܦܘܩ ܡܢ ܠܓܪ̈ܡܐ
ܡܢ ܠܒܪ̈ܐ ܠܓܪ̈ܡܐ ܡܢ ܓܪ̈ܡܐ ܠܒܣܪ̈ܐ ܡܢ ܒܣܪ̈ܐ ܠܓܠܕܐ
ܠܣܥܪܐ ܡܢ ܠܡܫܟܐ ܡܢ ܡܫܟܐ ܠܛܘܦܪܐ ܪܩܐ ܘܪܚܩܐ
ܒܫܡ ܐܒܐ ܘܒܪܐ ܘܪܘܚܐ ܕܩܘܕܫܐ ܒܫܡ ܡܪܝ، ܡܫܒܚܐ
ܡܪܝ، ܐܦܝܢ[6] ܒܒܢܝܐ ܚܝܐ ܕܡܠܟܐ ܪܒܐ ܒܡܠܟܘܬ
ܡܪܝܫ ܠܡܫܒܚܘܬܐ ܐܡܝܢ

[1] Short for ܒܐܘܪܚܐ.
[2] MS. ܗܘ̈ܬ.
[3] *Cf.* A, § 37.
[4] Evidently the word meant.
[5] The ܫ not quite clear in MS.
[6] Is this perhaps ܐܘܠܝܢ?

ܫܒܝܢܐ § 18 (sic) ܐܘܬܪܫ ܡܢ ܡ̣ܢ ܡ̣ܢ : (sic)

. . . . . § 19

---

¹ Just as the ܪ, ܙ and ܟ are almost indistinguishable in some places of this MS., so here and in other parts it is almost impossible to distinguish between the ܩ and ܡ.

² Have we the correct reading in this passage?

³ The heading and opening words are wanting in the MS. (*Cf.* A, § 23, and B, § 9.)

ܠܐܡܪ ܟܠܒܝܢܘܬܗܐ ܐܝܬ ܠܐܝܣܪ ܠܐ ܩܕܝܫܐ ܡܘܬܐ
ܘܡܒܣܪ ܟܣܐ ܐܘ ܠܥܠ ܟܣܐ ܘܡܣܟܝܐ ܟܣܐ ܢܝܟܢ.ܕܟܣ
ܐܡܒܬܐ ܐܟܒܢ ܘܢܫܡܐ ܟܣܠ ܠܐܗܠ.ܠܥ ܟܣܐ
¹(sic) ܐܟܡܪ.ܕ ܟܣܠ ܐܪܟܐ.ܕ ܟܣܠ ܘܡܣ ܠܐ ܘܟܡܒܐܪ.ܕ
ܟܣܠ ܟܣܕܝܕܝ.ܕ ܟܣܠ ܟܣܩܫܘܡ.ܕ ܟܣܠ (ܟܣܕ) ܟܣܒܝܕ.ܕ (ܟܣܝܒ
ܟܣܠܡܘܬܗ ܟܣܠ ܟܣܠܝܟܝ ܟܣܠ ܐܕܝ.ܐ ܟܣܟ (ܟܣܝܟ
ܘܕܝܘܚܘܪ ܟܣܠ ܟܣܣܡ ܟܣܩܝܡ ܕܠܗܡ.ܐܘܗܠܡܢ ܟܣܠ (ܘܝܚܘܪ)
ܟܣܠܟܪ.ܕ ܟܣܠ ܟܣܠ ܠܥ.ܠܗ ܟܣܠ ܟܣܒܡܘ.ܕ ܟܣܠ
ܘܟܣܝܐ ܟܣܠ ܟܣܒܘܡܗ.ܕ ² ܟܣܬܡܒܬ.ܕ ܟܣܠ ܟܣܝܒ ܟܣܝܒ
ܘܡܣܘܡܒܒܐ ܟܣܠ ܟܣܒܩܦܗ.ܕ ܟܣܪܐܒ ܒܡ ܟܣܡܢܗ ܒܡ ܬܒܠܡܗ ܒܡ
ܬܗܘܡܢ, ܒܡ ܬܗܬܡܗ ܡܡ ܡܡ ³ ܠܗ ܠܠ ܡܓܕܡ ܐܘܒ ܠܒܪ ܠܚܣܡ
ܟܣܪܒܐ. ܗܘ ܠܡ ܐܡܪܡܝ

§20 ܕܝܬ.ܕ ܟܣܒܡܒܐ ܒܡ ܕ ܟܣܝܠܝܣܣ

ܐܘܪܝܒܐ.ܪ ܟܣܠܘܠܡܠ ܟܣܕܝܬ ܒܡܬܟ ܟܣܒܝܬ ܟܣܗܒܪܐ ܐܒܡܢ
ܟܣܡܗܐ ܒܡ ܣܝܣ ܟܣܝܒܐ ܟܣܠܘܦܒ ܠܦܡ.ܕ ܟܣܒܝܒܘ.ܕܕ ܒܡ ܟܣܡܘܗ
ܘܟܣܒܡ ܐܡܒ ܠܚ ܟܣܝܒ ܟܣܝܬܐ ܠܥ ܡܒܣ ܣܘܗܒ ܟܣܒܡܘ

§21 ܟܣܐܝܬܗ ܟܣܠܘܟܣܐ

ܒܡܒ ܒܣܡ ܟܣܐܪ ܟܣܒܝܪ ܟܣܘܘܝܐ ܟܣܒܡܘܣ.ܕ ܟܣܡܒܬ ܗܡܒܢ ܘܝܨܬ.ܕ
ܐܘܦܗܩ ܟܣܪܒ.ܕ ܟܣܕܝܝܚܬ ܒܝܪܗ ܐܒܡܓܝܬܘܝ.ܘܒܝܘ ܒܝܪ ܟܣܪܒ ܟܣܐܒܝܣ ܣܥܐ
ܒܡ.ܗܡܘܣ.ܕ ܟܣܠܟܠ.ܪ ܡܕܗܒ ܗܒܡܣ ܟܣܒܝܘܪܐ ܡܕܣ ܡܒܠܬܠܗ ܐܒ
ܟܣܠܠܠ ܟܣܒܘܣܒܒܐ.ܪ ܟܣܒܒܪܐܡܝ.ܘܗ ܟܣܒܘܝܩܠ ܒܡܘ ܟܣܘܒܝ.ܬܠ ܟܣܗܦܒܘ.ܬ ܟܣܠܟܠ.ܪ
ܡܕܠܟܠ ܟܣܝܒ ܒܡ ܟܣܒܒ ܠܚܣܝ ܠܗܒ ܟܣܐ.ܗ ܡܠܬ ܗܡܒܠ ܒܣܡ
ܐܒ.ܕܝܝܬ ܟܣܒܠܟ ܐܡܒܟ ܟܣܒܘܣܕܐ.ܪ ܟܣܘܘܝܐ ܟܣܒܝܪ ܟܣܐܒ
ܠܗܒܡܒܬ ܟܣܐܒܝܪܐ.ܗ ܩܗ.ܘ(sic) ܪܝܪܝ :::::: ܟܣܠܟܠܐ ܘܒܝܪ,
ܒܣܡ ܐܡܒܟ ܐܒܡ.ܗ

---

¹ *See* note to Translation.
² This and the preceding word are underlined.
³ Delete.

(sic) ܚܢܘܒ (sic) ܚܒܘܪ ܡܣܐ ܡܣܘܐ ܠܐܕܡ ܡܣܘܐ ܘܐܠܐ (sic)
---

[1] *See* Translation.   [2] *Cf.* A, § 19.   [3] Evidently so.

ܐܣܒ̈ܗܬܗ ܢ̈ܕܗܝ، ܠܥܟܣ̈ܒܠ ܢܣ̈ܝ̈ܒܠܐ ܚܝܣ ܐ܀(sic)
ܠ̈ܡ.ܗ 5(sic)ܐ̈ܚ̈ܝ̈ܪ̈ܚ̈ܚ̈ܚ̈ܚ ܠ̈ܡ.ܗ ܐ̈ܚ̈ܟ̈ܪ̈ܐ ܝ̈ܡ̈ܬ̈ܚܐ ܐ̈ܚ̈ܗ̈ܝ̈ܚ̈ܐ̈ܚ̈ܗ ܠ̈ܥ܀
---

[1] Read ܐܣܘ̈ܚܝ̈ܐ, cf. B, § 7 heading.   [2] Perhaps delete final ܐ.

[3] Cf. B, § 7.   [4] Or ܒ̈ܪ̈ܐܩ.

ܐܝܟܐ ܐܠܝܘܣ[1](sic) ܗܕܝ܆ ܚܕܣܝ ܡܕܒܪܢܝܐ ܗܕܝ܆ ܚܕܣܝ
---

[1] l. ܐܠܝܘܠܟܐ.   [2] Or ܕܢܘܪܐ.

ܕܗܘ ܡܠܐܟܐ (sic) ܗܢܐ ܐܕܝ ܕܡܝ ܡܠܐܟ̈ܐ (sic) ܡܠܐܟ̈ܐ

ܐܗܝܐ ܐܦ̈ܝ ܒܡ ܐܣܢܝ̈ܡ ܒܡ ܡܡ ܡܣܝܕܚܚ (sic)ܘܗܪܕܚܬܐ ܒܡ

---

¹ ܐ̈ܒܝܝ̈ܘ̈ܝ̈ or ܐ̈ܒ̈ܝ̈ܝ̈ܘ.

² Probably the beginning of following word.

³ This and next word should evidently be transposed.

⁴ Illegible ; some such word as ܐ̈ܪ̈ܘ̈ܣ̈ܝ̈.

ܒܝܢ ܠܥܠܡܝܢ ܢܘܕܐ ܗܠܝܢ ܒܝܠܘܬܗ ܕܡܪܝ ܒܘܪܟܝܫܘ
ܗܘܕܐ ܚܝܝܐ ܐܡܝܢ ܘܐܡܝܢ

ܬܪܒܐ ܕܐܘܪܚܝܐ § 29

ܒܫܡ ܐܒܐ ܘܒܪܐ ܘܪܘܚܐ ܕܩܘܕܫܐ ܐܠܗܗ
ܕܐܒܪܗܡ ܐܠܗܗ ܕܐܝܣܚܩ ܐܠܗܗ ܕܝܥܩܘܒ ܐܠܗ̈ܐ
ܕܐܒܗܬܐ ܒܐܝܕܐ ܕܙܢܐ

APPENDIX

THE MS. in the British Museum (Or. 6673) is, for all practical purposes, the same as my larger one, marked Cod. A in this volume. The variations will be indicated in this portion of the work. Speaking generally, almost all the headings are gone or smudged beyond discovery, while in some portions they have been restored in pencil or ink; in fact, the writing throughout is not as clear as that in A, and the format is slightly smaller. This accounts to a great extent for the larger number of pages in Cod. B. M., although it should be added that a few additional charms (some called in this MS. ܢܩܠ *talisman*, an expression which does not once occur in either A, B, or C), introduced towards the end of the MS., would make some difference in respect of the size. These addenda have also been printed here.

With few exceptions the order of the charms agrees in both A and B. M. However, A § 8 and § 22 are omitted in B. M. altogether, and B. M. § 11 is absent from A. Further, B. M. § 9 corresponds to A § 10, and B. M. § 10 to A § 9, thus § 9 and § 10 changing places; B. M. § 12 corresponds to A § 11, and B. M. § 14 to A § 12; from B. M. § 15 to B. M. § 22 inclusive, it is in advance of A in point of number by one, B. M. § 23 being again A § 23 and so on till § 54. It is here that the interpolation of the few short 'talismans' given below, occurs.

Now for details. The following are the chief points in which Codex B. M. (British Museum) varies from Codex A :—

§ 1, at the end of l. 3, B. M. adds ܪܒܝܢ.

§ 4. B. M. commences here, as in other instances, with the ordinary introduction : ܒܫܡ ܐܠܗܐ ܡܪܝܐ ܚܝܐ : ܘܚܩܣ ; it interrupts at the word ܒܐܪܒܥ, and distributes the passage

from ܕܝܢܝ‌ to ܐ‌ܒܪܝܡ between twenty-five squares, not thirty-six as in A.

In l. 5 from end, it has after ܘܐܚܝܕ the word ܐܚܝܕ, and the last word is spelt ܘ‌ܝܢܚܕ.

In place of first three words in l. 4 from end it has ܘ‌ܝܠܝ‌ܐ ܘܕܝܡܝ‌ܐ.

In l. 3 from end, before ܡܢ, B. M. adds: ܟܠ ܕܕܟܠ ܕ‌ܡ‌ܕܝܢܬܐ ܘܕܐܠܐ ܘܐܘܢ‌ܐ ܡ‌ܫ‌ܒܝܚ‌ܐ ܘ‌ܒܝܬܕܝܢ‌ܐ ܘ‌ܐܪܟܘܢ‌ܐ ܘܐ‌ܪ‌ܒܝܐ ܘܐ‌ܒ‌ܗ‌ܬܐ; it omits the words beginning ܟܠ ܕܕ‌ܟ to ܕ‌ܡ‌ܝ‌ܬ‌ܐ.

§ 6. B. M. adds in heading ܘܕܗ‌ܠܝ‌ܢ ܘ‌ܕܝ‌ܢ‌ܐ; it varies somewhat internally, adding ܘ‌ܕ‌ܠܗܝ‌ܢ to the names of functionaries; and it strangely substitutes for 'Alexander, son of Philip' ܩ‌ܘ‌ܢ‌ܣ‌ܛ‌ܢ‌ܛ‌ܝ‌ܢ‌ܘ‌ܣ (Constantine) as 'subduing the whole earth'.

§ 7. In l. 4 from end, B. M. has for the first five words ܐܝ‌ܟ ܘ‌ܗ‌ܘ‌ܐ ܡ‌ܢ‌ܡ ܦ‌ܐ‌ܪ‌ܐ; in ll. 3 and 3 from end, it has ܕ‌ܠ‌ܗ‌ܝ‌ܢ ܘܕ‌ܝ‌ܢ‌ܐ ܘ‌ܐ‌ܝ‌ܕ‌ܐ ܘ‌ܡ‌ܒ‌ܕ‌ܝ‌ܐ.

The ending is peculiarly different:—ܡ‌ܢ‌ܡ ܕ‌ܠ‌ܗ‌ܘ‌ܢ ܕ‌ܡ‌ܢ‌ܬ ܗ‌ܠ‌ܝ‌ܢ ܕ‌ܒ‌ܝ‌ܕ ܗ‌ܘ‌ ܐ‌ܡ‌ܪ‌ܝ.

§ 9, l. 2 from end, B. M. omits ܠ‌ܟ‌ܠ.

§ 10. B. M. repeats part, evidently a case of dittography, and also adds the passage which 'our Lord said to his disciples, Go to the garden and cut therefrom &c.', contained in A § 20.

§ 11. B. M. differs in detail.

§ 12, l. 4. B. M. has the correct word ܕ‌ܬ‌ܫ‌ܡ‌ܫ‌ܘ for ܠ‌ܘܝ‌ܬ‌ܐ.

§ 16. B. M. omits in heading ܘ‌ܕ‌ܗ‌ܠ‌ܝ‌ܢ, and also the last line.

§ 17. B. M. in heading places ܝܕܡܠ last; at the end, it has ܕܝܠܗ, omitting ܪܕܘܒܝܐܠ and adding ܘܩܪܒܐ, ܘܩܘܡ ܡܒܝܬܬ ܬܪ—this latter being characteristic of the endings throughout Codex B. M. Each instance will, therefore, not be referred to.

§ 19. B. M. in l. 3 has ܣܘܡܠܐ, for ܘܠܡ,; in l. 4 for ܡܘܠܝܐܪ it has ܕܘܣܘܘܪ,; in ll. 5 and 6 before ܣܠܡ ܣܠܐ and after ܠܠܠܣ it has ܝܢ̈ܪܝ,; in l. 6 ܒܕܘܣܕܒܡ is one word; in l. 7 ܪܘܣܒܝ̈ܕܘ, is without the initial ܪ; similarly with the initial ܐ of final word in line; in l. 8 ܕܝ, is omitted; in l. 9 ܠܝܠ only once; in l. 10 ܠܬܝ occurs instead of ܠܬܝܠܬ.

§ 20. B. M. adds at end of first line ܝܪܕܘܝܪ.

§ 21. The last two lines are omitted in B. M.

§ 24. The heading in B. M. is certainly preferable to that in A. It reads:—ܬܪܝܕܗ.ܡ ܪܘܣܘܪ ܣܝܒ ܪܐ ܣܝܒܕܡ.

§ 30. B. M. has, in heading, ܝܪܘܒܙܝܪ ܪܕܗܣܘܝܪ; it omits the ending beginning ܕܝܠܗ.

§ 31. B. M. varies somewhat; it has in l. 4 from end ܕܝܐܝܒ for ܕܝܠܐܝܒ, and omits the word ܣܠܝܪ in last line.

§ 35. B. M. omits the concluding instruction ܩܘܝ ܠܠ ܣܘܣܪ.

§ 36, l. 3 from end, B. M. omits ܡܡ and has its characteristic ending.

§ 38. B. M. omits in l. 2 the word ܠܬܝ.

§ 41. After ܕܘܣܝ B. M. reads as follows:—ܕܡ̈ܣܠ ܣܠܐܠܕ ܝܪܘܣܕܗ ܕܬܘܪܕ ܘܣܒܝܪܕ ܣܝ̈ܒܕ ܘܣ̈ܕ

ܕܩܝܡ̈ ܡܨܥܝܐ ܚܝܝܝܬ ܡܥܠܬܐ ܗܘܡ ܬܩܠܐܠܬ ܩܘܩ ܒܪܝܫܝ
&c. ܐܝܫܪܝܐ ܬܩܘܗ ܗܠܡ ܫܡܥܬ̈ܐ.

In circle, for ܣܝܠܐ ܣܝܠܬ B. M. has ܬܬ ܣܡܥܬ.

§ 42, l. 2. B. M. adds ܘܒܪܣܝܬܐ after ܘܠܒܪܝ; l. 5, in place of ܒܡܪܒ, it reads ܒܠܠܐ ܐܕܪ ܬܩܬ ܬܩܘܢܝܬ ܒܪܒ.

§ 44. In last line but one, B. M. has ܩܪܒܐ ܩܕܝܝܕ ܐܪܐܠ ܐܦܪܐ ܩܪܒܐ ܒܡܠܐ ܐܢܝܪ.

§ 45. B. M. in l. 4 puts ܐܡܣܣ first.

§ 48. B. M. adds at end ܐܪܐܠܢ ܐܪܐܪ ܒܪܝܢ ܚܠܒܝ.

§ 50. B. M. adds in l. 4, after ܐܬܘܪ the word ܐܪܒܠܢ, and its usual ending referring to Mary and John the Baptist.

§ 51. B. M. has this heading:—ܩܠܦ ܐܕܪ ܬܩܘܢܝܬ ܒܐܪܒ.

§ 52. B. M. adds at end of heading ܒܡܥܪܒ ܠܐܐ; in l. 8 after ܐܪܝܠܣ, it adds ܐܪܘܐܝܪ ܦܘܣܝ, ܒܪܐ; in l. 11 it omits Mar John ܐܬܪܫܝܒ; in l. 15 for ܐܚܠܙ it has ܐܩܣܝܪ; in l. 20 it omits ܝܨܘܠܐܪ; in l. 4 from end it adds ܐܪܒܐ, and has its wonted ending.

§ 54. The colophon of B. M. naturally differs from A, in point of date and persons. In place of the 30th of Tammuz, 2114, we have Codex B. M. was written in ܐܒܒ : ܐܒ ܘܠܒܪ ܘܣܪܐܪ ܚܝܒܐ : ܐܚܒܢ : ܐ ܐܪܒܪܒܪܣܝܢ ܒܣܝܒ, thus fifteen years later than A; it was undertaken . . ܒܪܝ ܠܐ ܦܘܪܐܪ ܐܪܝܒܝ ܒܪ ܦܘܣܝܒܠܢ . . . . .

In speaking of ܦܘܠܝܩܢܝ,ܒܪܐܢ ܩܘܠܠܠܒ, B. M. adds:—
ܐܝܐܫ ܒܪܐ ܐܝܐܫ ܐܩܦܣܝ ܩܕܗܠܝ ܐܚܘܝܝܢ ܐܝܡܣܣ ܦܘܝܪܐܢ ܐܝܦܘܝܣܐ ܩܕܝܝܣܒ ܐܚܘܝܒܪܢ ܐܬܘܝܐܠ

In the words towards the end ܦܠܚ ܪܘܝܘܐܝ ܒܐܪܙܘܐܕ,
B. M. adds after ܦܠܚ the words ܪܙܡܐ ܘܐܠܡܠ; and
in l. 5 from end, after ܪܙܡܘܐ, it adds ܐܢܪܙܘ ܐܡܪܙܐܠ
ܘܐܪܙܡܐܠܐ ܐܙܝܪ ܘܐܠܪܙܐ; in l. 3 from end, for
ܘܪܙܡ B. M. has ܘܐܘ; and in l. 2 from end, after ܘܐܝ
Codex B. M. has the following ending :—ܒܪ ܘܪܙܡ ܒܪ
In this section we have the following additional charms,
to which reference has already been made :—

ܪܟܒܕܒܐ ܘܗܒܐܬܐ ܪܢܒܠ ܥܝܕ ܕܐܕ ܒܐܘܠܠܝ ܪܟܒܕܒ
ܘܐܒܪܝܘ ܗܘܐ ܒܪܝܢ ܐܠܐ ܚܠܘܬ ܠܕ ܠܕܕ ܡܐܕܚܕܒ
ܒܒܐܟܝܬܘܕܒܐ ܠܠ : ܢ: ܐ: ܗ: ܘܡ ܒܝܡ ܒܒܠܢ ܟܠܗܐ ܘܩܪܬܐ:
ܘܡܘܠܟܒܐ ܪܒܐܚܝܒ ܒܝܡ ܒܝܢ ܚܢܐ ܐܠܢܐ : ܗܠܒܝ ܪܠܡܘ.ܡ̈ ܪܪܐ ,ܐܪܕܟ
ܘܚܘܐ ܟܠܝ ܕܒܝ ܒܝ ܪܟܪ ܒܒܪܗ ܪ ܒܘܚܒܟܘ ܪܟܝܐ ܐܠܟܡ

ܪܐܘܐ ܪܢܒܠܝ ܪܟܒ § 57

ܠܡܒܡܩ ܒܝܪܪ ܪܝܪ ܒܪܝܐ ܪܝܐ ܒܝܕ ܝܠܝ ܒܠܪܟܐܠ
ܘܠܒܡܟܒܠ ܠܒܐܟܡܒܠܘ ܘܪܒܐܝ ܪܒܘ ܒܒܘ ܒܪ ܪܒܚܝܒܘܐ ܒܥܪܘ ܪܒܝܒ
ܒܒܪܟܐ ܐܗܘ ܐܘܡܢ ܠܒ ܠܒ ܒܠܒܠܒܐ ܐܒܚܒܒܐ ܐܚܒܒ ܒܗܒܒ
ܘܒܠܠܐܒ ܐܒܠܠܒܐ ܪܒܠܒܐܢ ܐܠܪ ܠܒܠܠܒ ܒܝܒ ܒܝܡ ܒܝܪ ܪܪܒ ܘܐܡܐ
ܚܒܒ ܠ : ܐ: ܗ: ܢ : ܘܟܝ ܒܠܒ ܟܠܡܒ ܠܟܒܝܕ ܒܝܪܒ ܝܒܕ ܐܠܟܡ

. . . . . § 58

ܒܝܒ ܐܠܪ ܒܪܐ ܘܪܟܐ ܚܘܐܪ : ܪܗܡܐ : ܒܝܒ ܒܐܪܟܝ ܒܝܒ
ܒܚܝܝܒܘ ܒܝܘܒܐܩ ܒܝ ܒܠܒܕܡܡ ܒܝ ܐܠܟܐ ܟܠܕܒܚ ܒܝ ܪܝ ܠܟܠ
ܘܒܪܝܪܠ ܘܒܒܪܐܒܠ ܘܒܚܘܐܒܪܟܠ ܘܒܚܝܟܘܒ ܒܟܐܝܦܠܝܘ
ܐܘܡܚܝ̈ ܐܡܡ ܒܚܒܒܒܝ ܠܒܚܒܚܐܠ ܒܐ ܐܘ ,ܝܪ. ܒܝܡ ,ܒܐܢܒ ܒܝ
ܒܒܬ., ܐܘܪܩ ܐܘܡܐ ܝܒ ܝܒ ܠܕܘܐ ܐܘ ܒܕܐܚܒܒܒܐ ܟܒ ܪܟܠܐܘ
ܒܝ ܐܚܒ ܒܝܒ ܘܒܚܕܠܒ ܚܝܝܚܝ ܒܝ ܐܒܪܘܐܟ ܒܪܒܒܐܢ ܒܝܐܝܪ
ܒܒܒܒܚܝܝ ܒܝܒ ܒܪܝܐ ܐܠܐ ܚܠܘ ܐܠܚܝ ܪܩ̈ܡܡ ܠܡ ܐܠ :
ܪܝܒܪ ܐܠܒܐ ܒܝܡ ܒܬܐܚܝܘܘ ܪܢܠܠ ܒܐܒ : ܗ: ܐ:
ܘܒܠܥܐ ܐܠܒܠܝ ܒܐܒܚܟܒܘܘܝ ܒܚܒ̈ܒܟܒܡ ܪܠܚܒܝܬ.ܪܟ(sic) ܐܡܝ ܒܥܒܝ.ܘܘ
ܐܡܐ ܒܚܒܕܠ ܚܘܩܐܪ ܚܠܘ ܐܠܐ ܪܝܢ ܒܘܠܒܩܘ
ܠ : ܐ: ܗ: ܡ: ܒܠܒ ܠܒܬ ܒܬܝܝ ܒܬܚܝܝ ܒܝܕܪ ܪܟܕܘܐ ܐܡܪ ,ܪܒܘܝ ܒܝܒܝ
ܪܪܟܒ : ܒܚܒ ܚܠܝ ܘܚܘܘ.

ܠܗܕܪܝܢ ܐܠܐ ܫܝܐ ܕܐܪܬܬܐ ܕܬܗܡܬ܆ ܒܕܘܬ܆ (sic)
ܚܣܢܬ [or ܒܣܠܝܐ] ܕܐܠܗܬܐ ܗܗܒ ܠܠܟܕܪܝ ܒܪܐܟ
§ 61 . . . . .

ܐܝܢܪ ܠܗ ܡܠ ܠܠ ܆ ܐ܆ ܡ ܆ ܗ܆ ܡܒܐܪ ܝܪܐܩ [or ܒܣܠܝܐ or]

ܚܬܝܡ ܚܪܡܐ ܗܢܐ ܒܫܡ ܒܡܘܐܬܠ ܗܫܐ ܘܒܟܠܙܒܢ
ܘܠܥܠܡ ܥܠܡܝܢ

§ 63 ܕܪܘܫܡܘܬܐ ܕܟܘܪܐ

ܚܬܝܡ ܠܚܪܘܬܐ ܡܪܝܚܝܢ ܠܗ: ܒ: ܕܦ: ܝܠܗ ܡܪܝܐ
ܐܕܢܝ ܘܒܝܫܐ ܡܠܠ ܕܡܫܪܝܐ ܐܢܐ ܘܒܝܫܐ ܒܫܘ
ܦ̂ܘܪܩܢܐ ܕܢܫܒ ܠܢܘܐ ܡܢ ܐܠܗܐ ܕܕܦܢܘ ܕܐܕܡ
ܒܗܠܝܢ ܬܠܬܐ ܡܠܐܟܐ ܡܫܝܚܐ ܕܡܒܪܟܝܢܗܘܢ ܒܝܫܐ
ܘܡܪܝܪܝܢ ܢܘܟܪܝܬܐ ܠܗܬ ܦ: ܒ: ܕܦ: ܥܕ̈ܝ ܟܦܬܢ
ܥܠܘܗܝ ܘܢܬܪܣܢ (?) ܠܐ ܢܬܠ ܠܥܠܡ ܘܡܥܬܐ ܕܕܝܦܘܗܝ
ܘܠܐ ܠܬܥܠܡܘܗܝ ܢܗܘܘܢ ܡܬܕܪܐ ܐܝܟ ܠܫܒܘܬܐ
ܕܒܪܘ ܘܐܝܟ ܕܕܒܒܬ ܢܘܪܐ ܡܢ ܕܒܝܬ ܫܝܫܐ ܐܬܘܢܐ
ܕܟ̈ܠܝܢܐ ܘܠܐ ܬܬܘܩܕ ܐܝܟ ܘܠܥܪ̈ܟܠܝܗܘܢ ܗܟܢܐ
ܬܬܟܢܝ (sic) ܫܡܬܐ ܕܪܘܚܢܐ ܘܬܪܥܝܬܐ (sic) ܡܢ ܦ:
ܒ: ܕܦ: ܐܝܟ ܕܐܣܪ ܦܘܡܐ ܕܐܪ̈ܝܘܬܐ ܡܢ ܕܢܝܐܠ
ܢܒܝܐ ܘܠܐ ܚܒܠܘܗܝ ܐܫܬܢܘ ܦܘܡܐ ܕܕܘܒܐ ܡܢ
ܛܠܝ̈ܐ ܬ̈ܠܝܬܝܐ ܕܐܠܗܐ ܗܢܐ ܢܫܬܪ (sic) ܦ̈ܩܕܝܗܘܢ
ܕܐܢܢܝܐ ܒܢ̈ܝܐ ܡܢ ܦ: ܒ: ܕܦ: ܐܡܝܢ

§ 64 ܐܣܘܪܐ ܕܪܚܡܐ

ܐܡܪ ܦܬܓܡܐ ܡܢ ܡܪܢܘܬܐ ܕܕܘܝܕ: ܕܐܬܪܚܡܬܝ
ܘܪܚܡܬܟ: ܘܥܒܕ ܒܪܝ ܟܠ ܟܘܪܐ ܘܪܕ̈ܝ ܟܚܢܐ
ܕܢܣܐ ܥܡܘܠ ܥܒܕܐ ܦܪ̈ܕܐ ܕܫܢ̈ܐ ܒܢܝ ܥܠܝܗܘܢ
ܗܠܝܢ ܦܬܓܡܐ: ܗ: ܘܒܢܝܢ ܫܢܝܢ: ܘܒܢܝܢ:
ܘܐܠܗ: ܐܟܒܪ: ܚܠܡܬܝ: ܗܠܠ: ܘܠܕ: ܗܒܠ: ܒܗ:
ܗܫܠܡܝܢ: ܐܒ: ܕܘܘܕ: ܣܬܡܬ: ܒܣܬܡܬ
ܐܠܗܝܢ (ܐܐܠܗܝܢ or) ܐܪܒܥ: ܡܢ ܫܐܝܠܬ (ܫܐܠܬܐ or):
ܘܦܘܩܕܐ: ܘܐܠ ܡܚܝܐ ܐܝܬ ܠܗ ܡܬܘܐܐ ܕܐܪܒܥܝܢ . . .

ܣܡܪܐ (sic) ܐܘܫܒܐ ܘܓܢܠܠܐ ܓܒ ܚܕܝܢܠ ܓܝܬܪ ܐܠܬܟܐܪ

ܘܪܓܘܗ، ܚܣܒܘܪ (sic) ܚܕܕ ܓܒ ܐܝܟܠܐ ܒ : ܒ : ܕܗ:

ܐܪܒܝܕ ܣܘܒܕ ܩܗ ܡܠܣ ܒܚܘܐܣ ܗܠ ܟܠ ܬܕܬܐܩ (sic) ܪܠܬܒܐܕ

I add here B.M. § 11 which is also wanting in A:—

For EU product safety concerns, contact us at Calle de José Abascal, 56–1°,
28003 Madrid, Spain or eugpsr@cambridge.org.

www.ingramcontent.com/pod-product-compliance
Ingram Content Group UK Ltd.
Pitfield, Milton Keynes, MK11 3LW, UK
UKHW010337140625
459647UK00010B/657